Advance Praise for
Runaway Husbands

Vikki Stark provides women whose husbands have left them abruptly an invaluable guide to understanding what has blindsided them, and offers the healing kind of help that comes from hearing stories of survivors of this often overlooked form of spousal abuse: abandonment.

– Louise DeSalvo, Ph.D., author of *Writing as a Way of Healing*

If you marry Dr. Jekyll and get Mr. Hyde and he walks out the door with no warning, then this is the book for you. Stark's "Seven Steps for Moving Forward" are right on and will get you back on the path—or, as she suggests, move you to an even better one.

– Catherine Gildiner, Ph.D., author of *Too Close to the Falls, After the Falls* and *Seduction*

Runaway Husbands is a wonderfully moving and informative book that will help thousands of women, as well as the men who have the courage to read it.

– Jed Diamond, Ph.D., author of *The Irritable Male Syndrome: Understanding and Managing the 4 Key Causes of Depression and Aggression*

Vikki Stark shares her personal story, along with the stories of many others she interviewed, and guides the reader through the difficult stages of recovery. This hopeful book shows not only how to cope but also how to claim yourself again.

– Constance Ahrons, Ph.D., author of *The Good Divorce* and *We're Still Family*

For Lauren and Michele,
of course

RUNAWAY
HUSBANDS

*The Abandoned Wife's Guide
to Recovery and Renewal*

VIKKI STARK

Green
Light
Press

This book is an original publication of Green Light Press
Montreal, Quebec
Canada

For information, contact:
Green Light Press
vikki@runawayhusbands.com

Library and Archives Canada Cataloguing in Publication

Stark, Vikki
Runaway husbands : the abandoned wife's guide to recovery and
renewal / Vikki Stark.

Includes index.
ISBN 978-0-9864721-0-7

1. Divorce. 2. Divorced women--Psychology. 3. Divorced women–Life
skills guides. I. Title.

HQ814.S735 2010   306.89'3   C2009-907531-8

The names of the women who participated in The Sudden Wife
Abandonment Project have been changed to respect their privacy.

Contents

Acknowledgements

Writing a book with the help of four hundred co-authors is truly a pleasure. You—the Sudden Wife Abandonment Project participants—opened your hearts to share with me perhaps the most painful and intimate time of your lives, either by contributing a questionnaire or face-to-face interview, posting on the *Runaway Husbands* website or even just by writing to me. The sense of solidarity among us all runs deep. I thank you for trusting me with your stories.

My circle of friends who supported me so that I could keep going with this project also deserves a super-sized "thank you." Your names should be engraved in stars on the *Walk of Fabulous Friends!*

Heartfelt thanks to Nili Baider, Sandy Grossman and Catherine Mauger. Jeanette Limondjian was always available to encourage and guide me in endless ways, including the book production end of things. Andrea McElhone and Carolyn Badger, dear friends and colleagues who read the manuscript with a red pen and critical eye, helped me clarify my thinking about the dynamics of human behavior. Lynn Williams acted as a sounding board for many of the ideas in the book as well as insisting that *Runaway Husbands* had to be its title. You were so right!

My colleague in the field of mid-life men's psychology, Jed Diamond, was tremendously encouraging and generously shared with me what he's learned from his own research and publishing experiences. Sandra Phillips, Stan Posner and Emma McKay acted as my mentors in small press publishing, turning a very overwhelming prospect into a manageable set of tasks.

I am grateful that Adrian Zimmermann, my very own project manager, sauntered into my life early in the development of this work, sharing my delight in the creative process. Thanks for your passionate interest in the project and for insisting that I always aim for excellence.

Michele and Lauren Goldman—when I think of you, I feel both happiness and hope. It's been a luxury to have two very talented daughters with whom to talk through every aspect of this book. I've depended on your balance, perspective and good sense to guide me. And thank you, Michele, for your keen editing advice. Profound appreciation to you both.

Runaway Husbands

Wisdom from my mother's friends:

"Dare I venture to say that, judging from my own life
experience over the years, I have found that sometimes things
that happened to me that appeared destructive from the outside,
have eventually turned out to be very constructive things that
I myself did not, at the time, have the wisdom to foresee."
LILLIAN WACHTEL

"I hope this 'interruption' in your life will not turn you into
a weakling, but that it will lead you to a new beginning and
a life that will be even happier than the last twenty-one
years have been."
IDA COOK

CHAPTER I

My Husband, the Hologram

The fall of 2006 should have been one of the happiest times of my life. My first book, *My Sister, My Self*, had just been published and I'd just completed a book tour speaking at bookstores and community centers across the United States about sister relationships, the subject of my book. Planning the trip, I'd envisioned how great it would be out there driving the open road alone, listening to local radio stations and getting the chance to talk with dozens of women about a topic dear to their hearts. Although the reality of driving three thousand miles across America proved to be much more challenging than I'd expected, at least I had backup. During our nightly phone calls, my husband of twenty-one years was cheering me on, telling me how proud he was, always encouraging me.

After three sometimes very lonely weeks on the road, I took the red-eye back east from California, stumbled off the plane and fell into my husband's arms in tears. I was so relieved to be home, so happy to see him. There was only one more event on the book tour later that week, and it was the one I was most eagerly anticipating—my official book launch in Montreal where I live. All my friends were coming (some flying in from New York), as were the press, my colleagues and many of the women who participated in The Sisters Project that formed the basis of my book. We were expecting close to a hundred people. It was to be my triumphant return—the best day in my life!

When we returned from the airport, my husband dropped me at home and rushed right off to work, which I found a bit odd; usually he loved to stop for coffee and reconnect whenever one of us returned from a trip. I took a shower and noticed a long dark hair in the bathtub but thought little of it. Later, however, when I was on the phone with my longhaired daughter, I asked as an afterthought, if she'd been at the house recently. She said no, not while I was away. Then I forgot about it.

I spent the day unwinding from the trip and enjoying the anticipation of the upcoming book launch. That evening, when my husband arrived home from work, I threaded my arm through his, gave him a squeeze and said, "I bought fish." He looked at me rather strangely and said, "It's over." I stared at him and asked, "What's over?" vaguely thinking that that was a weird way to say that he didn't want to eat fish anymore. He answered, "The marriage. It's over. I'm leaving you. I'm moving in with my girlfriend." Horrified, I watched the words take shape in slow motion as they left his mouth and hang in the air before they crumbled. Pow! Shock! I'd spent twenty-three days on the road only to be hit by a Mack truck in my own living room.

My husband had *never* mentioned that he was unhappy or thinking of leaving me. During the previous months, he'd signed greeting cards with endearments like, "I love you with all of my heart," "Thank you for the myriad joys you bring me" and "You are the rock of my life – then, now, always!" Until the moment of his revelation, I was deeply in love and believed him to be, too. Had you tapped me on the shoulder five minutes earlier and asked me to describe my marriage, my eyes would have misted up as I rhapsodized about how my husband was the most loving, attentive, and trustworthy man any woman had ever married and how lucky I was to have found him. In other words, *I'd had no idea*!

I'd trusted him completely not only because of how bonded I thought we were after the many difficult life events we'd weathered so well together (my mother's Alzheimer's, his health problems and liver transplant), but also because he had always presented himself as the personification of morality and decency. Integrity—that's what everyone believed he stood for. It was inconceivable that he'd been lying and betraying me for what I soon learned were six long years.

He went on to tell me details that I neither wanted nor needed to hear. He said he'd broken up with his girlfriend five years earlier when he learned that he needed a transplant because he wanted me to take care of him, but he got back together with her as soon as the wound healed. Two years later during his sabbatical, she was with him in South Africa although in his phone calls he'd constantly declared how much he missed me and how lonely he was. The "solo" Vermont hiking weekend that he'd excitedly described to me in such detail while I was on the road had actually been a romantic getaway. His girlfriend had been at my house, cooking dinner in my kitchen and sleeping in my bed, while I was out there on the book tour.

Being a therapist, I knew right away that the marriage was truly over. I didn't fight or challenge him. I sat quietly as my husband revealed all this to me in the most brutal way possible, with no preparation, no logical explanation and no remorse. He made no acknowledgment of the magnitude of what he was doing or of the life we'd shared. I hate to sound dramatic, but it felt like he'd stuck a knife in, turned it and then watched dispassionately as I sat there bleeding. I'd always been the one to protect and comfort him when he was hurting. Now, I was on my own.

I was completely traumatized. My body was thrown into an uproar; the emotional pain was physical and almost unbearable. My mind jammed as I struggled to redefine the happily married reality that had been a fact of my life for decades, and integrate a new vision of my husband. It was as if he were a hologram. His face looked familiar, but the man standing before me was in reality a stranger.

He wanted to leave immediately, but I asked him to stay until I had a little time to process what was going on. He spent the night on the sofa. The next day he threw all his belongings into garbage bags and bolted from my life directly into the arms of his girlfriend.

The Sudden Wife Abandonment Project

That's my personal account of what took place at the moment of my husband's dramatic departure from our marriage. But although I was in the throes of the most traumatic event of my life, a part of me was also standing back, observing from the vantage point of a trained professional. I'd been a marriage and divorce counselor for over twenty years and in the course of my practice had witnessed a number of marriages dissolve. As a matter of fact, around the time that my husband said he had started his affair six years earlier, I had just co-founded a counseling center dedicated to helping families cope with divorce.

I was measuring what I'd observed with clients against what I was experiencing in my own life, and I just didn't get it. Most people assume that it's impossible for a person to have an affair without the partner having some knowledge—that the injured spouse is always either complicit or purposefully blind. However, that was not my case. Under even the closest scrutiny, I was unable to discern any trace that could have tipped me off that things were not hunky-dory in the marriage. On the contrary, few wives could boast of a more devoted mate, and, oddly enough, until the revelation of his infidelity and subsequent heartless flight from the marriage, he was the ideal husband!

I just couldn't wrap my mind around how a man who genuinely appeared so committed to our marriage could morph overnight into an angry stranger. In the midst of my suffering, I knew that there'd be no rest for me until I could figure it out. So as days stretched into weeks, I started researching wife abandonment. Through reading and speaking with other women, a remarkable picture slowly started to take shape; my husband's bizarre behavior seemed to fit into a pattern exhibited by other men who suddenly bolted from apparently happy marriages and then turned against their wives. The similarities were uncanny! I defined this pattern and named it Wife Abandonment Syndrome (WAS).

Time and again, the women I spoke with recounted the same details in describing their husbands' flight from the marriage, from the exact words spoken to announce the end and his post-separation behavior to the type of woman he chose as an affair partner. So, as I'd done for my Sisters book, I decided to conduct a study to learn more. I established a website, www.runawayhusbands.com, on which I provided information, a community bulletin board and a questionnaire about WAS (a copy is located in the back of this book), and also started interviewing women face-to-face. Soon the stories started pouring in.

Before I knew it, the Sudden Wife Abandonment Project (SWAP) was off and running! I'd heard from over four hundred people by the time I stopped collecting interviews. SWAP participants were mostly women who'd been left, but I also received questionnaires from children whose fathers had fled, men who were abandoned by wives and even some of the runaway husbands themselves.

Women who visited the website were deeply relieved to know that someone could shed some light on the nightmare they'd been going through and were eager to help in any way they could. Here are some of their comments:

- "I went to your website and wept when I read some of the posts and the pieces of advice. I'm not sure people have truly understood what I have been going through until I read some of the information on your site."
- "Your website has been a source of support to me during this time. I never believed my husband would 'run away' and felt so demoralized when he did. It's helped me to know that other women have gone through what I'm going through now. It's comforting to know that I'm not alone."
- "It made my day to read about your research and to hear your take on WAS—so familiar to me. So many people cannot believe that this can just happen without obvious signs— and it does. It happens even *with* signs that lead you to believe your marriage will last forever. It is such a confusing

and devastating event—I hope that your book will be of
help and lessen the feelings of self-doubt and inadequacy
that can prevail for so long."

- "I was really shocked when I read the article in the newspaper [about WAS] as it perfectly mirrored my story. I hope
that by telling my story I can help you to help us understand
this, grow and move on."

I Will Be Your Sherpa

Wife Abandonment Syndrome is a pattern of behavior that begins
when a husband leaves his wife out-of-the-blue without ever having told her that he was unhappy or thinking of leaving. Following
his dramatic revelation, he replaces the tenderness he'd typically
shown her with anger and aggression. He often moves directly in
with a girlfriend, leaving his bewildered wife totally devastated.
This will undoubtedly be the defining event in her life, and although
recovery is a struggle, many women find that it forces them to rein-
vent themselves in positive and enriching new ways.

You picked up this book, most likely, because at some point in
your life, the same Mack truck that hit me hit you, and you want
answers. Not only do you need to know what happened, but,
more important, you need to know *what to do* about what happened. Whether your husband left last week or last century, you
yearn to put that chapter of your life to rest, once and for all. That
doesn't mean that you won't think about him with emotion—
you're human after all. It just means that you won't think of him
as often and, when you do, it so won't hurt so much. Once you've
worked through your recovery process, thoughts and feelings
about your marriage and former husband will lose their power to
disturb you as profoundly. You will be able to reflect on it without getting the sick feeling that you had in the months after your
husband left.

It's hard to recover when you've been betrayed by the person
you trusted the most. You were seared to the bone and have to fig-

ure out how to rebuild your life, starting with your self-esteem. There are few people who really understand what you're going through or can counsel you, even within the therapeutic community. It will take all your resources to move beyond the pain, obsessiveness, anger and general misery to the next part of your life. This book will guide you through the stages of recovery so that you don't get stuck, and it will give you a vision of how, in spite of it all, you *can* have a much better future than it's possible to imagine right now.

The crisis of abandonment is first and foremost a crisis of identity. Much of what you took as a "given" about yourself and your world has been thrown into question. Feeling loved by your husband gave you a sense of self-worth as you saw yourself reflected in his appreciative eyes. When he rejected you, your first reaction, rather than anger at him, was probably to feel badly about *yourself*, internalizing *his* vision of you and tallying up the ways in which you weren't the wife he wanted. But when you regain some perspective, you will see, if you haven't already, that a woman doesn't have to be perfect to be a good wife. If he was unhappy, he owed it to you to include you in a discussion of his feelings.

Now that the marriage is over, you'll need to stop taking your husband's assessment of you as the right one. You'll need to learn to value your own view of the kind of wife you were, and the woman that you are. That takes courage. It's much easier to depend on others to inform you about yourself than to trust your own opinions. You need to learn that just because someone else believes something about you, it doesn't necessarily make it true.

Like it or not, you will have to change in many ways in order to adjust to this new reality. Here are some of the emotional tasks you'll need to complete:

- Revise your beliefs about human nature. You now have learned that some people are capable of deception.
- Believe in your self worth. You must stop feeling discarded, empty and less valuable than the woman who has taken your place or than married women in general.

- Get accustomed to being self-reliant and independent.
- Expect good things in your future. Don't assume that you will always be alone or miserable.
- Stay positive! Stop yourself from becoming bitter or developing a victim mentality.

I know you can turn this traumatic event into an opportunity for growth and change. Once you understand what happened to you and accept the fact that your life is not going to unfold as you'd planned, new doors will open and you will realize that your future is in *your* hands. Hearing the stories of SWAP participants, I was astounded to learn how many of them bounced back, redefining their lives and launching off in new, unexpected directions. In spite of the hurt, anger and sense of loss, in spite of the injustice of it all, in the final analysis it's up to you to decide what to do with the new life you have been given. But first, we have some work to do to bring you to that point.

Here's what Elizabeth Gilbert wrote about happiness in *Eat, Pray, Love*:

Happiness is the consequence of personal effort. You fight for it, strive for it, insist upon it, and sometimes even travel around the world looking for it. You have to participate relentlessly in the manifestations of your own blessings. And once you have achieved a state of happiness, you must never become lax about maintaining it, you must make a mighty effort to keep swimming upward into that happiness forever.

As you embark on this journey, I will be your Sherpa. I will carry the supplies and do the heavy lifting, but you must walk with me along the path. We'll stumble. We may have to double back sometimes. But in the end, we can enjoy the view from the top of the mountain with the satisfaction of knowing that we fought hard to get there.

Hallmarks of Wife Abandonment Syndrome

1 Prior to the separation, the husband had seemed to be an attentive, emotionally engaged spouse, looked upon by his wife as honest and trustworthy.

2 The husband had never said that he was unhappy or thinking of leaving the marriage, and the wife believed herself to be in a secure relationship.

3 The husband typically blurts out the news that the marriage is over out-of-the-blue in the middle of a mundane domestic conversation.

4 Reasons given for his decision are nonsensical, exaggerated, trivial or fraudulent.

5 By the time the husband reveals his intentions to his wife, the end of the marriage is already a fait accompli, and he often moves out quickly.

6 The husband's behavior changes radically, so much so that it seems to his wife that he has become a cruel and vindictive stranger.

7 The husband shows no remorse; rather, he blames his wife and may describe himself as the victim.

8 In almost all cases, the husband had been having an affair. He typically moves in with his girlfriend.

9 The husband makes no attempt to help his wife, either financially or emotionally, as if all positive regard for her has been suddenly extinguished.

10 Systematically devaluing his wife and the marriage, the husband denies what he had previously described as positive aspects of the couple's joint history.

CHAPTER 2

Transformational Stages

Recovery from WAS doesn't follow a linear path. Sometimes you may feel that you've really made progress only to have the breath knocked out of you by a vivid dream or a song on the radio. You'll measure the time since he left and get impatient with yourself—"Why aren't I over it already?" Friends will insist that you need to move on or tell you formulas that are supposed to prescribe the amount of time during which it's acceptable to grieve. Don't listen to them.

We are all different and our own unique backgrounds will determine how we react to any of life's experiences. Although you may have the support of family and friends, you're going to have to do this your way—there's just no other option. Most people find that recovery takes longer than they thought it would. It's very important to cut yourself some slack if you're still working through it years after your husband left. It's a complex process to renovate a reality that you may have spent decades constructing.

Here's a rough meteorological description of the **Transformational Stages** that you can expect to go through during your recovery process. Remember that you'll certainly bounce in and out of them and that they will be peppered with good days and really rotten ones. The value of being able to define where you are and track your progress is twofold. First, you'll see that there is some structure in the midst of the chaos and that will make you feel more secure. Second, you'll realize that no matter how badly you feel, it's just a stage in the healing process, which won't last forever, and that will give you hope! Take a look at the eight stages below and plot where you think you are at the moment:

- **Tsunami**—You take the first hit when you are informed out-of-the-blue that the marriage is over. You feel like you're drowning and go into shock.

- **Tornado**—Your thoughts are spinning wildly as you try to come up with some desperate plan to make this not be happening, or at least to understand it. It's a crazy and dangerous time—you're not in your right mind.

- **Thunderstorm**—You feel attacked, raw and fearful and don't know when the next thunderbolt will strike. Your emotions ricochet wildly from anger (lightning) to grief (rain) to fear (wind).

- **Ice Storm**—Life feels hard, cold, unrecognizable and unforgiving. You've lost your footing. There is no future and time slows way down. You're frozen, just trying to make it through each day. You wonder if you'll ever feel normal again.

- **Fog**—Your interior world is still gray, but the feeling's not as intense. You've grown profoundly tired of struggling with your emotions, but your mind is slowly starting to function again.

- **Sun Shower**—The world has started to thaw and regain some color as you begin to seesaw between bad days and good.

- **Early Spring**—Although there are still traces of all you've suffered, new opportunities have started to bud. You feel your life gearing up for change.

- **Warm Summer Day**—You have made the transition into your new life and look to the future with anticipation. You've learned how to create your own happiness.

Not Your Typical Divorce

What makes Wife Abandonment Syndrome so devastating for a woman is not merely that her husband decided unilaterally to leave the marriage. Rather, it's the way in which he does it. The fact that his departure was completely unanticipated, and that his wife believed herself to be in a good marriage, makes it so destructive. Although the woman being left certainly contributed to whatever problems existed in the marriage, the important fact is that she was blindsided and lied to by her spouse, who had a secret agenda. There *are* some things in this world that are black and white, right or wrong, and it's just not fair for a man to walk out on his wife without having let her know her that her marriage was on the rocks.

In a typical divorce that is not affected by WAS, the marriage may have been faltering for months or years. The couple probably was bickering and fighting, or suffocating in the vacuum of stony silence. The kids were painfully aware that things between their mom and dad were not good. Sex most likely flew out the window as the tension mounted. When things got really bad, they may have tried marriage counseling. Threats of divorce were probably hurled about in fights. When the end finally came, they were both so battle scarred that a bit of relief may have been mixed in with the sadness.

But a divorce affected by WAS is not at all typical. Here are the ways in which it differs from the more common unwanted end of a marriage:

1 **Shock Value**
The woman being abandoned is completely unprepared, not only emotionally, but also in concrete ways, such as finan-

cially and with regard to work-related decisions and
child-care. She's caught completely by surprise.

2   **A Sense of Powerlessness**
When a woman sees the end of her marriage on the horizon,
she has some notion that she can affect the course of
events—by suggesting couple's therapy, reading a self-help
book or trying to revive the marriage in some way. But when
a woman learns that her marriage is ending only after it's
already over, she's not a part of the process and is completely
powerless.

3   **Lack of Closure**
A wife who continues living with her husband during the
dying phase of a marriage has the chance to talk with him
about what she's going through because they're still together
in the house. In Wife Abandonment Syndrome, she's robbed
of the opportunity to say anything at all—he's often already
gone!

4   **Deception**
In almost all cases of WAS, the husband has been having an
affair. He also has the luxury of secretly making preparations
to protect himself, long before informing his wife of his
plans.

5   **Reality is Shaken**
What the wife had thought of as a "given" in her life—that
her husband is an honest man who cares deeply about her
welfare—is destroyed when she learns that he has been
playing a role that made him *appear* to be a loving, engaged
spouse. When the truth is revealed, she finds it hard to trust
her own perception of reality.

6   **A Redefined Past**
The end of any marriage deeply affects a woman's present

and future. In Wife Abandonment Syndrome, the woman left is forced to question events from the past as well. Due to the affair, she's driven to do the detective work of trying to figure out what was really going on. She struggles to make sense of her husband's revisionist story of their life together because he now recasts it in a negative light—very different from her lived experience.

7 **Greater Effect on Children**
Children are deeply disturbed and more likely to feel abandoned because they had no warning that their father might leave. It causes them to question their own sense of reality. The presence of the affair partner significantly alters the relationship with the father.

8 **Greater Effect on Friends**
The couple's whole friendship network is often shaken up, as people weigh in as to who was to blame. Friends start to examine their own supposedly solid marriages, thinking, "If her husband, who appeared so happy, could leave, why not mine?"

Georgia, 41 years old, whose husband had left six years prior, provided an example of how he redefined her past and how she went along with his revisionist story of the marriage, until she was able to retrieve her own version of their joint history:

At first I accepted his revision of our marriage and I went back and mentally X-ed out any good memories I had of him or our time together. My hatred for him ate me up, consumed me, for years. Then one day I picked up the watch I'd worn every day of our marriage and had stopped wearing the day he left. It was a watch he'd given me as a wedding present and it had his initials and our wedding date inscribed on it. I took it to a jeweler and asked if the inscription could be etched out. He said no, it could not, impossible. I took it to a different jeweler, same answer. I did this three times and finally came home so frustrated that I was about to try and scratch the initials out myself.

Suddenly I looked at that watch and it hit me that maybe I was having no luck getting rid of it for a reason. Maybe I didn't want to lose the inscription. It was a real "light bulb" moment and the point at which true healing began. The inscription became a symbol for the restoration and honoring of my own memories of my marriage and my husband, whom I had deeply loved.

That man died the day he left me and was replaced by a person I've never had positive feelings for, someone I don't even know. I co-parent with him as best I can and otherwise avoid him. But nothing and no one will ever again touch the memories I have of the husband I loved and the marriage I put my heart and soul into. From a place where I least expected it, this perspective brought me a peace that had eluded me for so many years. Now I look at that inscription to remind myself of the husband I loved. It's a good feeling every time.

You can hear how Georgia struggled to transform the anger that was eating her up into a state of mind that would allow her to retrieve the memory of the tenderness that existed in her marriage. She experienced that as a turning point in her healing process—the "light bulb" moment in which she permitted herself to reclaim former feelings of love. But, that realization didn't change her current guarded attitude toward that same man.

You see how complex it is! Although her marriage had ended long before, Georgia still needed to do a huge and demanding piece of emotional work in order to stop being consumed by her anger. It permitted her to honor the love she felt for her former husband during her marriage but remain wary in her present dealings with the same man, whom she no longer trusts. She wrestled with terribly bitter feelings and found a way to move beyond them. Only when she was able to integrate the fact that she felt two conflicting emotions about the same man, could she achieve a feeling of peace.

To get there, she needed to accept that although her husband had changed, the love she *once* felt was real. That's the heart-breaker! Emotionally, it's less painful to say that the whole thing was a lie than to embrace the fact that it was once wonderful and then, incredibly, it changed and was irretrievably lost.

The Seven Steps for Moving Forward

The months following the revelation of WAS may well be the hardest time of your life. Abandonment of this magnitude is trau-matic—every aspect of your life is affected. You are tormented by your thoughts; your emotions are out of control. You have an awful, sick feeling in your body. While you are in the midst of it, it's virtually impossible to believe that this suffering will ever end. Life is a relentless struggle, and there's only one word to describe what you're going through—misery. I know. I've been there.

You may think to yourself, "People endure far worse atrocities in this world—I should stop complaining." It's true that horrible things do happen, but that doesn't diminish the life-altering and profound nature of what you're going through. The fact that your life has been thrown into chaos by the very person with whom you've had an intimate connection, the person you depended upon to love you and comfort you, injures a deep internal sense of safety.

We learn to trust even before we are born. Trust defines our connection to the person, usually a mother, who must care for us and keep us alive. Without it, a helpless infant would be at terri-ble risk. To enter into as intimate a relationship as marriage, we also need a rock-solid conviction that the person that we are welcoming into our inner world is worthy of our trust. Once we have that assurance, we can re-create the primitive bond we once had with a mother, which permits us to feel safe enough to let down our guard. When we suddenly learn that the person we depended upon to maintain our safety not only has left us unprotected, but also has intentionally harmed us, our very first lesson in life—that it's safe to trust others—is challenged.

In *The Journey from Abandonment to Healing*, Susan Anderson compares the experience of the sudden loss of love to that of going cold-turkey from a drug addiction: "Love withdrawal is just like heroin withdrawal, involving intense craving and agitation for the love you are missing. You ache, throb, and yearn for your loved one to return. Human beings are genetically heir to a powerful need for attachment; severed relationships do not end your need to bond. In fact, losing your relationship tends to intensify this need."

Re-establishing the belief that it's safe to trust again is an arduous process, made even more challenging if you've had other breaches of trust in your life growing up. Those women who survived childhood abuse or abandonment, which they struggled to overcome in order to put their faith in their husbands, are even more profoundly injured by WAS. What helps in recovery is identifying other reliable relationships with people whose love has remained unshakable across time. Although the intimate love of a marriage partner is often seen as primary in our lives, the value of a dependable bond with a parent, sibling, child or friend can go a long way toward helping you heal.

You *can* move forward, and many women advance to a better place, creating a new life that is freer and happier—one that makes them proud. The **Seven Steps for Moving Forward**, which are necessary to accomplish in order to recover, permit you to disengage emotionally from your former husband, accept your new reality and gain the confidence to face life as an independent person. They are:

1　Recognize that the chaos won't last forever (needed to resolve the Tsunami Stage).

2　Accept that the marriage really is over (needed to resolve the Tornado Stage).

3 Integrate the fact that your husband has changed irrevocably
   and is beyond caring for your welfare (needed to resolve the
   Thunderstorm Stage).

4 Understand why he needs to justify his actions any way
   possible—including rewriting history, lying or attacking
   you (needed to resolve the Ice Storm Stage).

5 Give up trying to get the acknowledgment and apology that
   you deserve (needed to resolve the Fog Stage).

6 Turn your focus from the past to the future (a step in both
   the Sun Shower and Early Spring Stages).

7 Celebrate your new life as a single person (Warm Summer
   Day Stage).

I know from personal experience that these **Seven Steps**,
although necessary, are not easy to accomplish. Theresa, who read
about them on the Runaway Husbands website, recently emailed
me about her struggle trying to move through them:

> Your Steps above ...
> Maybe #1, I can do.
> But #2, I just can't seem to (almost two years now).
> 3 is a given, despite not believing 2.
> 4. Yes, understandable.
> 5. Don't expect one.
> 6. Easier said than done ... he was both.
> 7. I hate being single. There is NOTHING to celebrate or
> gain from it.

Two years post-separation, Theresa is still very much in the
thick of it. She can *maybe* recognize that the chaos won't last forever, which means that she still feels her life is pretty chaotic, but
she can't seem to accept that the marriage is really over. In spite

of not believing the marriage is over, she knows that her husband has changed and is no longer interested in her welfare. She does understand why he needs to justify his actions but doesn't expect an apology. And her husband was both her past and her future— she's having trouble embracing her *new* life without him. She hates being single! Emotionally, she's fighting the profound change that happened in her life, tooth and nail.

To accomplish Steps 3, 4 and 5, you need to develop an understanding of what happened—how did your husband's feelings suddenly change, and why did he flee from the marriage instead of including you in a discussion about it's demise? I don't presume to know specifically what happened in each case of WAS, but having done a lot of thinking, discussing and researching about this topic, I'll share with you my thoughts about why some husbands end their marriages in this dramatic manner.

CHAPTER 3

Dr. Jekyll and Mr. Hyde

Strange Case of Dr. Jekyll and Mr. Hyde, a novella by Robert Louis Stevenson, fascinated nineteenth-century English audiences because it explored the concept of the duality of human nature—how both good and evil can co-exist within the same person. When we call someone a "Jekyll and Hyde," we infer that he "is vastly different in moral character from one situation to the next" but keeps that difference well hidden, perhaps even from himself. He presents his socially acceptable side to the world, the Dr. Jekyll side, and splits off the Mr. Hyde side from his consciousness, denying it and burying it deep inside. The tension of keeping that shadow side hidden becomes increasingly intolerable until it bursts out in a destructive release.

I have heard from many abandoned wives that the man who walked out on them was not only a nice guy, but also a spectacular husband—extremely affectionate, seemingly deeply devoted to his family, often the pillar of the community—a pastor, doctor, professor, Little League coach who was beyond reproach. Many described their husbands as unusually romantic, men who were the envy of the wife's women friends. People would look at the couple in envy, marvelling that they had it all.

Recently, researchers from Northwestern University in Illinois explored the connection between a person's sense of moral superiority and his or her comfort in doing wrong. They came up with some very surprising results. Rather than finding that those who believe themselves to be unusually good are more altruistic than others, the researchers found the opposite to be the case. People who assess themselves as exceptionally good cut themselves more slack in certain situations and may even give themselves license to act unethically. It's the "I gave at the office" mentality—"I've already done so many good things, you don't expect me to be perfect, do you!" Similarly, men who run away from their marriages may feel that their former good reputation should be enough to excuse this current little transgression.

From my analysis of the hundreds of SWAP interviews, I've come to believe that WAS men often have very ambivalent feelings toward women. They need their wives desperately, putting them on a pedestal, but deep down hate the very fact that they need them so much—that hunger makes them feel too vulnerable. Their fragile self-esteem requires unconditional approval. The husband may experience the simplest criticism or complaint voiced by his wife in the normal flow of living together as a devastating attack. The unsuspecting wife appears to her husband to be very powerful, and he fears her unwitting ability to make him feel small and powerless.

This likely results from the man's childhood relationship with the mother, whose approval little boys crave. Our society socializes boys differently from girls. While girls are not only permitted but also encouraged to remain emotionally attached to their mothers throughout their lives, the same closeness in boys is seen, very early on, as unhealthy. The term "momma's boy" is a put-down, and boys are careful to hide that attachment for fear of being labeled weak or possibly gay. But that doesn't mean that boys don't need the tenderness and support of their mothers every bit as much as girls do. They're stuck with an inherent paradox— if they seek out their mother's warmth, which they need in order to feel secure, they risk having their very identity as a male questioned. If they distance from their mother, which society encourages, they may feel frightened and small. Anthropology professor David D. Gilmore, author of *Misogyny: The Male Malady*, was commenting on men's intimate relationships with women in this quote, but it has equal value as a comment on a boy's need for his mother: "So man must cling helplessly to woman as a ship-wrecked sailor to a lifeboat in choppy seas. He desperately needs her as his salvation from all want and from oblivion; his depend-ency is total and desperate. But, and here's the rub, man must also separate from woman to achieve anything at all. He must over-come his desire to regress to infantile symbiosis with her if he is to be accountable as a man."

Gilmore's observation helps us understand the origins of the intense and ambivalent relationships some men have with women—they were excluded from their mother's protection too early. The damage is intensified if there is a sister in the family who was permitted to remain bonded with the mother while the boy, feeling like an outsider, looked on jealously.

Protector to Persecutor

Madeleine Bennett, author of the 1991 book *Sudden Endings: Wife Rejection in Happy Marriages*, wrote about how husbands who abandon are filled with self-loathing and, in order to toler-ate those feelings, "project" them onto their wives. The men delude themselves into believing that it is the wife who hates *them* and that she is trying to bring them down. Bennett writes, "This justifies unquenchable anger and continuous punishment of their wives for being carriers of the bad parts of themselves they wish to disown." Further, she talks about how her own abandoning husband had changed: "Arthur the Protector had metamorphosed into Arthur the Persecutor, an adversary who could not bear to be in my presence, whose every utterance insulted our past and threatened my future."

Prior to leaving, men who eventually run away seem to have a very idealized view of marriage and look to their wives to pro-vide them with the good stuff they need to enhance their self-esteem. When a man hits the inevitable midlife bump in the road and comes face-to-face with the fact that his power is on the wane, he may subconsciously blame his wife for not protecting him from that blow to the ego. As his disillusionment with himself builds, so does the case against his wife, who is often at the height of her powers in midlife. Some part of him recognizes that his resentment is unjustified so he harbors it in secret, building up grievances in his own mind until they eventually reach a tipping point. Then, to preserve his identity, the decision is made to escape from that person whom he perceives as causing his diminishment.

While he was "in" the marriage, it was in his interest to downplay his mounting anger. But once he decides to leave, he feels justified in his need to try to destroy the "depriving" wife. He has to leave fast, running, to avoid further damage to his self-esteem caused by his "powerful" wife. He must tear her down as much as possible on his way out the door so she'll be too devastated to fight back.

Madeleine Bennett's description of her husband's grievance against her illustrates how he perceived her as purposefully depriving him: "Arthur's complaints about our marriage contained one fixation, the pervasive, unshakable conviction that he had never gotten his way. He felt martyred. The concessions and compromises that to me had reflected normal give-and-take between two reasonable people to him represented total surrender to a demanding, manipulative wife."

I experienced the identical thing! I had a lot of respect for my husband's opinion and assumed that he was right in most cases. I'm a pretty easygoing person and we rarely fought. If I occasionally disagreed with him about something, he'd often counter with, "There you go again, making me into the bad guy." I'd be so surprised that he could see it that way that the comment usually stopped me in my tracks and I'd back down. If one of the kids concurred with something I'd said, no matter how trivial, his stance would be, "You're ganging up on me." If I brought up an issue more than once, he'd shut me up by saying, "You're badgering me." I was always flabbergasted. Sometimes, the last time I'd mentioned the topic was months or even years prior, but if it crossed my lips a second time, he'd accuse me of harping on it. He was unable to tolerate any criticism and made it seem as though I was attacking him if I raised anything at all. He somehow had the conviction that I was running the show when, in reality, everything revolved around him.

I used to joke that my husband was so affectionate that he couldn't walk the ten steps from the house to the car without holding my hand. After he left, I struggled to understand why he showed no remorse and seemed to have no regard for my welfare when, during the marriage, he appeared so over-the-top adoring. I eventually hit upon a metaphor that helped me—his powerful attachment to me was of a parasitic nature. He needed me so desperately, "sucking" on me for dear life, not as a beloved separate individual but as a nurturer who existed in his life solely to provide him with an identity and fill his emptiness. When he'd finished with me, he jumped to the next "host," his girlfriend. He reattached just as firmly to her, fusing with her and taking on her identity, suddenly despising what he stood for when he was married to me. I'm sure that he again appears to be a loving husband, as devoted to his new wife as he was to me.

My Book Launch

So what did I do about my book launch? Remember, my husband left me three days before it was scheduled to take place. What was I going to do? There was no way I could cancel it. Dozens of women who had participated in the Sisters Project had been looking forward to it, and I really didn't want to disappoint them. Plus, the bookstore had ordered over a hundred copies of my book. But more important, I'd worked for three years on that book. I was very proud of it. My husband had just taken so much away from me, I'd be damned if I was going to let him take this too! I knew I had to go ahead with the launch and do what I'd done at bookstores all across America. But I also knew that if I was going to pull it off, I couldn't have all my friends asking me where he was on the night. I had dedicated my book to *him*! I was not going to lie.

Most spouses who have been dumped don't typically get on the phone and immediately inform everyone they know of the news. But, during those three days, I had to telephone all my friends to tell them why my husband was not going to be at the launch. It was undoubtedly one of the hardest things I've ever had to do. Over and over, our outraged friends asked why, after a six-year affair, couldn't he wait a few more days in order to let me have my moment. But I was still a long way from accessing that anger. At that point, I was just stunned and hurt.

In many ways, my book launch *was* my greatest triumph! I don't know how I got myself into the frame of mind that made it possible, but I gave a funny, heart warming reading, which my audience enjoyed. The women who had participated in the Sisters Project didn't realize that there was anything wrong. My daughters and friends who at first were terribly worried for me quickly saw that I was going to pull it off. Many had tears in their eyes as they watched me tell funny stories and talk about my book. The bookstore manager and staff were cheering me on. The whole thing turned out to be a love fest!

I was in an altered state. At one point in the middle of my talk, the thought flitted across my mind that I sorely wished my husband could have been there with me to celebrate. That reverie so distracted me that I lost track of what I was saying and briefly panicked. But I managed to bluff my way through and no one caught on. In the photos, I look normal, but if you look carefully, you can see my younger daughter's protective hand on my shoulder. It was a wild and successful launch—the culmination of a painful, strange and intense initial stage and the start of a challenging new chapter in my life, one that would require all of my skills to master.

The aim of this book is to help you understand what happened to you and figure out what to do about it. Reading the stories of other women who experienced Wife Abandonment Syndrome will aid in clarifying what you're going through. You're sure to see your own experience reflected in their words, and that will make you feel less alone. My analysis of WAS will provide structure to this chaotic time in your life. But understanding is not enough. I'm determined to help you turn this experience around into something meaningful and profound and will guide you with workable techniques and effective strategies to make that possible. **The Big Fridge,** stocked with coping tricks and recovery strategies, is located in Chapter 10 if you need a sneak peak to tide you over.

Here's what three SWAP participants said about the growth they achieved as a result of having been left:

- "I often tell people that I would go through it all again to be where I am today. At first I felt like the dumb housewife who was dumped for the bright assertive woman. However, I was given so much support from my closest neighbors and friends. I actually gained a higher self-esteem. Also, after taking a college course to get back into the workforce, which was followed by more courses to upgrade in my jobs, I realized that I was not stupid and if I put my mind to it I can accomplish anything!"

- "It is still the saddest thing I've ever lived through. I have still not gotten over it. I have however, gotten around it. I felt very poorly treated at the ending of my relationship. Sometimes, I still can't believe he did it. What a bum! However, I do feel an immense sense of freedom, of lightness and lifting. I am my own person. I try to live my life in kindness. Maybe I am just now recognizing this tremendous feeling of lightness."

- "I went into the depth of my being and saw how strong I am. I'm really strong and I know it. Nothing can break me in the same way—I mean, it didn't break me! I know that no matter what's in front of me (and I've had difficult things), I'm very strong and all I need to do is to go deep into my place and I'll be okay."

CHAPTER 4

Amputation without Anesthetic

One fall afternoon many years ago, I had the strangest experience. I was heading home from work on the New York City subway, glad that I found a seat because I couldn't wait to get back into *Shogun*, the novel I was reading at the time. Transported to feudal Japan, I counted the stops in the back of my mind without looking up while I sat engrossed in my book.

Arriving at my station, I sprinted out of the subway, still absorbed by my book's tale, but when I reached the street I was stunned by what I found. My familiar corner had somehow morphed into an alien landscape. Instead of the shops and street I knew so well, the scene I encountered was beyond recognition. What had happened? Panicking, I wondered if I'd slipped through the cracks into an alternate reality. Would I ever be able to find my way back home? Had I gone mad?

My mind scrambled to come up with a logical explanation for this bizarre transformation, and very soon it clicked. In my eagerness to get to my book, I'd jumped on the express train instead of the local, overshooting my station and ending up way beyond my stop. As soon as I realized my mistake, the world stopped whirling and I calmed down. Chuckling to myself, I did a U-turn and headed back down the subway steps, happy for the chance to steal a few more minutes of reading on the return trip south.

Welcome to our world! When your husband of a decade or two suddenly says, "It's over!" that moment of relief—realizing it's all a mistake—never comes. You *are* locked in an alternate reality. The landscape *is* unrecognizable, and you *have* become a stranger in a strange land.

The Revelation

- "It was a Friday night at the end of July, just three days before our son's thirteenth birthday."
- "I was told at 5 p.m. on the 6th of February."
- "He sent an email just before midnight Chicago time on November 8, 2006."
- "On October 3, 1991, I got up at 5 a.m. to get ready for work, went to the kitchen to start the morning coffee and discovered a note from my husband."
- "He telephoned me from the office just after lunch on Tuesday, September 14, 2004."
- "At 6 a.m., Sunday, October 16, Mike got up to go to work. I asked, 'Will you be home for dinner tonight?' and he said 'No.' And then he said, 'I'm not coming back.'"

In interview after interview, participants in the Sudden Wife Abandonment Project pinpointed the exact moment their life skidded off course. No matter how long ago it occurred, the details remain indelibly stamped in each woman's mind—where she was standing, what she had been doing, what was said, the level of light in the room, the smell of coffee brewing. It all remains real and tangible, lodged forever in her sense-memory. She will relive that traumatic moment over and over relentlessly in the months that follow, trying to extract some meaning from it, but no matter how often she dissects it, it never offers up any answers. The reworking will develop a mythic quality as the bewildered wife cannot stop herself from obsessing about it, like Sisyphus condemned for eternity to roll the boulder up the hill only to watch it inevitably slip back down. She keeps returning to that moment on what one woman called the "Day of Devastation" in the hope that, if she could just figure out what happened, she might find a way to be released from the torment.

For some SWAP participants, that moment arrived with the brutal surety of the plummet of a guillotine—gruesomely described as "amputation without anesthetic." Like myself, these wives were completely oblivious to the fact that their marriage was in jeopardy until they were informed that it was already over. Not having had any suspicions, they were living their lives in blissful ignorance. With zero preparation for the dramatic events about to unfold, they were completely blindsided.

For others, the end came as "death-by-a-thousand-cuts." These women had also thought their marriage was secure, but before their husband reached the point of lowering the boom, they became aware that something was amiss. They are the ones who stumbled across text messages, hotel receipts or love letters while rummaging through their husband's desk for the extra key to the garage. They then were compelled to take on the job of detective, embarking on humiliating days or months of sleuthing, possibly punctuated by accusations and denials, until the moment he finally declared, "It's over."

In both types of endings, the wife is an innocent bystander to the wreck of her marriage. The fifth Hallmark of Wife Abandonment Syndrome is evident: "By the time the husband reveals his intentions to his wife, the end of the marriage is already a *fait accompli*." The husband makes the decision unilaterally, news of the end is delivered suddenly, and long before the words leave his mouth, his wife's fate is sealed. She has no say in the matter and no idea how she got there.

Guillotine Style

The surgical precision of the "guillotine style" of ending, although more shocking, is easier in some ways than the "death-by-a-thousand-cuts" method because the wife is forced to accept the finality of the event. Nathalie, a physiotherapist from Seattle, was 49 when her husband, Jim left; he was 51 and a manager in a pharmaceutical company. They'd been married twenty-two years and had two school–aged daughters. Nathalie described her marriage as follows: "I loved my husband and our life together—I thought he was my best friend. I adored him; we had a wonderful life, beautiful home, lots of fun and laughter." She characterized her husband's personality as "very generous, kind, cheerful and positive." She knew that Jim disliked confrontation and avoided discussing problems, but looking back, she thought that everything "was fine," so Nathalie was flabbergasted when he suddenly announced it was over.

> I was working on my computer, charting my appointments for that day. He came up to me and said, "I'm leaving." I continued typing and said, "Oh yeah? Where ya' going?" thinking he was going on a hike or maybe a business trip. He said, "No, I'm leaving." I looked up at him with shock beyond any descriptive word in any vocabulary, with a profound, unbelievable look and with utmost sadness, and said "Oh, Jim." I will never forget that moment or that day for the rest of my life. I felt ripped, blown up, shattered beyond any description, in utter, utter shock—I COULDN'T believe it.

The eerily casual manner in which Jim announced the end of their twenty-two-year marriage was typical of how many runaway husbands deliver the news. One would think that a decades-long intimate relationship deserves a more ceremonious send-off. You'd expect a more serious discussion even if the pair had been just dating for a few months! For example, Jim might have said, "Nathalie, please come into the living room. I need to talk to you," or, "Could we take a walk tonight? There are some things we need to discuss," or, "I don't want to upset you, but I've got something important to tell you." Jim's offhand declaration suggests a bizarre attempt on his part to deliver devastating news in a way that Nathalie would not take too seriously. Maybe if he could just slip it into a mundane conversation, she wouldn't notice. I call this the "out-of-the-blue" method of marriage dissolution.

Here are some other examples:

Heather—28 years old, married seven years

We got up one Saturday morning, preparing to go to the market. He was sitting on the bed in his boxers, putting on his socks, and he said something like "I can't do this any-more," and I had no idea what he meant. The market? Shopping?

Jennifer—43 years old, married twenty-three years

Allan blurted out he was leaving me last November while he was drinking a cup of coffee and I was doing dishes. I thought I hadn't heard him correctly.

Abigail—38 years old, married fourteen years

He came home from "union negotiations" on a Saturday. I asked him if he wanted a glass of wine, and he said, "I can't do this any more." I said, "Drink wine?" He said he wanted out of the marriage.

Anita—42 years old, married four years

One afternoon, he called me from work and there was a standoffish tone in his voice. We spoke briefly about nothing … no argument, just small talk and then he said, "I can't do this anymore." I said, "Do what anymore?" suspicious, but thinking he must be talking about this dumb conversation we were having. And he said, "I can't continue this relation-ship anymore." And I said, "What? Why? What do you mean?" And he said, "I just can't." And that was literally the last conversation I ever had with him. He came and took his things while I was at work. He never took any of my phone calls. I never got an answer about why this was happening. I never even got another glance in my direction from him.

The end of my own marriage followed the same pattern. When my husband replied, "It's over" to my statement that I bought fish, I literally had no idea what he was talking about. Why were I and all the other women to whom this happened so confused? Because the end of the marriage was such an unlikely explanation for our husbands' statements that it was literally unthinkable.

But why were our husbands making their announcements as a *non sequitur*, seemingly expecting us to know what they were talking about? Because the plan to leave had been foremost in their minds for some period of time, and they somehow assumed that their ever-attentive wives, who cared so much for their welfare, must have been magically *au courant* to the monumental decision. It was glaringly obvious to the husbands that the marriage was dead, and they were sure their wives would see it the same way. As SWAP participant Tahira said, "He'd left me six months before—he just forgot to tell me!"

Joseph Hopper, a researcher from the University of Chicago, wrote an insightful article, "The Symbolic Origins of Conflict in Divorce," in which he talks about how the one who leaves needs to redefine the marriage. He says that initiators must "undo the sacred" as a way of justifying their decision. They accomplish this feat by "reconstruing their marriages into 'marriages that never were.'" He writes, "Rarely did I hear someone explain a divorce solely in terms of an affair ... Instead, they came to see their difficulties as being deeply rooted and their relationships as suffering from 'structural flaws.'" Hopper goes on to say, "With a focus on the negative and an emerging sense that their marriages were flawed and phony, initiators understandably saw divorce as inevitable. Divorce became the obvious, natural, fated, and logical outcome of the past." The abandoned party may have had a totally different experience of the marriage, but to the initiator, it was clear as day. As a result, "initiators were disappointed, even baffled, when non-initiators did not agree with their assessment and, in fact, opposed their efforts."

It is surprising how many men end their marriages using the same phrase: "I can't do *this* anymore." The "this" refers to "continue pretending that I'm in this marriage." Being in a couple demands such a degree of closeness that the strain of keeping up the pretence eventually reaches a point at which even a master compartmentalizer realizes he can't continue. He had been working through the idea of leaving over a period of time. At first it may have seemed impossible because he still defined his identity as part of the marriage. But little by little, with the encouragement of his girlfriend, leaving his wife became more feasible, until one day he woke up and it was not only possible, it was inevitable. The novelist Russell Banks analyzes this process as follows: "The husband believes that he's been deceived, fooled or seduced by his wife and now the scales have fallen from his eyes and he can see the truth of the situation." The husband has worked through any hesitation he may have felt about launching into this exciting new venture by accentuating in his mind the negatives associated with the marriage, until it becomes intolerable to remain with his wife, even for another day.

He hadn't thought through, however, what a friend of mine referred to as the "law of unintended consequences"—how his news would affect and, more important, change his wife. He severely underestimates how his behavior will harm her as a person; he's so focused on himself that her reality doesn't much enter into it. What he cares about most of all is that she doesn't make it hard for him to extricate himself.

Before announcing their intentions, men who run away often suffer in silence. They don't express their mounting dissatisfaction because they're conflict avoiders, but that avoidance of conflict just covers up a stew of unspoken resentment that one day bubbles over. While still performing the role of ideal husband, although he may be living a double life, he had a vested interest in keeping that resentment to himself. He'd do anything to avoid his wife's wrath. However, once the decision is made to leave and leave quickly, there's no holding back the unexpressed anger that may have been pent up for years.

Death-by-a-Thousand-Cuts

In "death-by-a-thousand-cuts" endings, the process unfolds through agonizing fits and starts, with the bewildered wife lurching on a roller-coaster ride from despair to hope to despair again. Nadia, 38 years old, tried for weeks to figure out what was going on with Sean, her husband of seven years, but he kept declaring that everything was fine. However, when she confronted him with irrefutable evidence that he'd been having an affair, rather than agreeing to work on the marriage, he shocked her by revealing that he already had one foot out the door.

Asked how she would have described her marriage, Nadia said, "Solid. We have always been a good 'team,' worked together and never fought. We always talked and had great communication (or so I thought!)." Here's the story of how it all fell apart.

It started in mid-December when I got the "feeling" something was amiss. He assured me everything was OK. Then I found something on the computer (him on an Internet dating site) and he explained that away. It was a plausible explanation, so I believed him. I still felt things were "off," but I decided to wait until he returned from a business trip after the New Year to see how he was toward me. The night he came home, he gave me something to read on his work computer. There I found another document chronicling his dating exploits for the past few weeks. This included him asking my friend for another friend's phone number. He told her that our relationship was over and he was moving out in two weeks. I had been oblivious. Around that same time, he was making me a surprise birthday party, and although he was behaving like everything was fine, he had already rented an apartment.

After I found the document, I simply went to him and said, "So, when are you leaving?" He said, "For what?" and I said "Forever." He just hung his head and said, "Tuesday." This was Sunday evening.

Although Nadia's marriage ended out of the blue, she had an inkling that something was brewing. Similar to women who experienced the "guillotine style" of WAS, she thought she was in a good marriage. Her husband's dissatisfaction was never expressly articulated, but once he decided he wanted out, she had no say in the matter. He had already rented an apartment by the time she put the pieces together.

Here are other examples of marriages that ended through "death-by-a-thousand-cuts"—when the wife confronted her husband after deciphering of clues:

Sharon—47 years old, married twenty-three years

He had a female "friend" that was the age of our youngest son. I found emails from her in which she declared her love. When I asked for an explanation, he said I misinterpreted it. I still have not received an explanation for how I can misinterpret, "Hello, my love, I love you. You know me every way imaginable. I am not complete without you."

Valerie—39 years old, married eighteen years

My husband told me he was working and would not be home until late. I decided to stop by his office to bring him some supper, but he wasn't there. In fact, the lights in the whole building were off. I sat there and waited until 10 p.m. to see if he would return. He never did. He came home around 11:30 p.m. I asked him whom he was with. He said "nobody"—that he had gone out for supper and he went shopping afterwards. I knew he was lying.

Suzie—53 years old, married twelve years

One weekend, he was in the most sour mood I've ever seen—EVER. It was like he was a different person. No longer would he hold my hand or cross the street with my elbow in his hand. There was zero affection or care and a lot of hostility. I kept asking him what was wrong, to which he would reply "nothing." Another couple of hellish weeks went by, and one night I opened the credit card bill. I saw two hotel charges. Everything went white. I literally got dizzy and was STUNNED. Everything became foggy. All the little things I had been noticing came rushing back to me and I couldn't believe it. Then I opened up the phone bill, which includes cell phone charges. I highlighted the numbers I didn't recognize and began to call them. When he came home, of course, he denied everything and made up an elaborate story to explain the charges and the phone calls. He left that evening and never returned.

By leaving a broad trail of clues that compel the wife to be the one who initiates the rift, the husband can get the ball rolling without even having to broach the subject. It's a way of exiting the marriage by the back door. And because the presence of clues forces the wife to play detective, many husbands express outrage at their wife's snooping, giving them a perfect excuse to get angry with *her*. That diverts the focus from the affair to the misdemeanors the wife had to commit to uncover the truth, illustrating the principle that the best defense is a good offense. Women get confused because they have such a tendency to feel guilty. They permit the focus to be redirected from their husband's big transgression to their own very small one.

A second type of ending via "death-by-a-thousand-cuts" occurs when, although the revelation of the affair has been made, the husband takes some time to finally leave his wife. Sometimes the timing of this interregnum is really in the service of his girlfriend's process of extricating herself from her own marriage. During that time, the wife is often subjected to a cruel challenge—"If you pass the test, I might stay."

In her memoir *Madam Secretary*, former U.S. Secretary of State Madeleine Albright described the events around her husband's sudden departure in a classic case of Wife Abandonment Syndrome à la "death-by-a-thousand-cuts." After his announcement that he wanted out and although he was living with his girl-friend out of town, the marriage was still stumbling along. Albright recalled, "The next months were a unique brand of torture. Obviously Joe had meant to be decisive, but once he got to Atlanta [with his girlfriend] he evidently felt either less certain about what he was doing or more uncomfortable about the way he had done it. So he called me—daily. He loved me, he loved me not. He actually described his feelings in percentages. 'I love you sixty percent and her forty percent,' or the next day, 'I love her seventy percent and you thirty percent.'" You can only imagine what that constant weighing of her worth as a woman and wife did to Albright's self-esteem. Although wives whose marriages end in this way do have the opportunity to do some processing, the experience of having failed the most important test in their lives leaves them worse off than those who didn't even know that they were being evaluated.

CHAPTER 5

Out the Door

Calling It Quits by Blackberry

Unbelievably, a certain number of men in the study told their wives of their plans to leave by phone, email, text message or even post-it note! Several broke the news by having one of the children inform their mother. Gina, 51, was driven to the airport by her husband, Fernando, when she left for a week's vacation with their daughter. He kissed her good-bye, wished them a great trip and said he'd be there to pick them up when they returned. That was the last she saw of him.

> When we arrived home, my son was there instead, saying that his dad had been sent out west on an indefinite assignment with his company. "Very strange," I thought. Fernando contacted me by email a few days later, sounding odd. A week later he phoned, sounding really strange. I emailed his son in Albuquerque, describing this situation and asking if he had any details, to which he responded that he knew nothing. A couple of weeks later, however, his son wrote again saying that his father had informed him of our split. This was totally shocking and a huge surprise to me. My ex had never informed me of it.

Pauline was notified by her husband of twenty-five years that the marriage was over with a note on the kitchen counter: "It was a Saturday and I had a pancake breakfast at school. I called about 2 p.m. and he gave me a grocery list and everything seemed fine. When I got home at 4 p.m., no one was home. I found two envelopes on the counter in the kitchen; one addressed to me, and the other, for our son. In mine he said that he had to leave, we didn't have much in common any more. He had left before I got the news."

Lindsay was sent an email while her husband was away "working" in the Yukon. She writes, "He said he was not happy, that he had given up on our relationship and was 'on a new journey.'" And Sue wrote, "I had just taken him to work and everything was fine between us—he kissed me and told me he loved me. Then two hours after a phone call telling me again how much he loves me, he sends me a text message telling me that we're through and that I'm to leave the truck, the bank information and get out."

Although "cowardly" is a common descriptive for all the guys who suddenly and without forewarning abandon their wives, "cruel" would be more accurate for those who can't summon up the guts to tell their wives to their faces. And rough as it is for women who are told face-to-face that their husbands are leaving *now*, it's a thousand times harsher to be left without the chance to respond even with a word. Women who have been victims of a "hit-and-run" revelation feel robbed of *any* opportunity to defend themselves, adding another layer of complexity in recovery.

Sagittarius and Capricorn Don't Mix!

Although some husbands say "It's over" and bolt right out the door, those who stick around for a few hours or days usually are pressed by their wives for an explanation, in what often develops into an agonizing discussion and fight. The wives who told me their stories rarely said that the reason their husband gave actually clarified his motivation for ending the marriage. On the contrary, the justification given was typically completely mystifying and caused the woman great grief as she replayed it endlessly, trying to extract a particle of meaning from something that is inherently nonsensical.

The fourth Hallmark of WAS is: "Reasons given for his decision are nonsensical, exaggerated, trivial or fraudulent." Departing husbands typically concoct explanations that are quantifiable, irrefutable and "true" in the hope that they will satisfy, but those excuses in no way match the gravity of the decision to end a marriage. Here's a sample of reasons given to wives in the Sudden Wife Abandonment Project by departing husbands:

- "He said, 'You left too many shoes by the back door.'"
- "He listed a bunch of ridiculous reasons such as when he went grocery shopping I had listed Tide on the wrong place on the list and he had to circle back to get it; he wasn't happy that we had got a second dog; there was a flower in a vase that he thought should have been thrown out; there was a spot of food on the kitchen counter that had not been wiped up."
- "We had recently moved to a new town. His reasons for leaving were vague—'I can't stand the drivers here,' 'I can't stand the employees here.' "
- "He said we did not need Scooby-Doo, our year-old Boston Terrier!"
- "My husband told me that he left because of my knee. He is addicted to climbing and after my knee surgery, the surgeon said that my climbing days were over."
- "He said I didn't share the same retirement plans."
- "He finally realized after thirty-eight years of marriage that Sagittarius and Capricorn just don't mix."
- "He said it was because his daughter called off her engagement last summer. If she'd gotten married, he would have stayed."
- "He said that I brought up too many personal stories at dinner parties and it was affecting the intellectual quality of the conversation."
- "The reason he gave for leaving me for her? She was more religious than me. And yes, the religion is one where adultery is considered a sin."

Madeleine Albright described her husband's bizarre justification for his decision. During the months following his revelation, while he was making up his mind which woman to choose, he was in the running for a Pulitzer Prize in Journalism. She recalled, "Joe grew fixated on winning. One day he came up with a startling proposition: If he got the Pulitzer, he would stay with me. If not, he would leave and we would get a divorce." The day he found out he didn't get the Pulitzer, he *did* leave. Albright writes, "I could never make sense of the possibility that my marriage might have been saved if only the Pulitzer committee had made a different decision." In some mystifying feat of mental alchemy, he exported all responsibility for his choice to some external agent, so it would be possible to claim, "It's not my fault—I had to leave! I didn't get the Pulitzer!" Although clearly absurd, such explanations are offered as diversionary tactics. It's just too hard to say, "Some younger woman looks up to me, finds me attractive and we're having hot sex. It's just too good to pass up!"

Abandoned wives, desperate to make sense of their husband's reasoning, find the bizarre justifications excruciating. Many say that is the lack of any sensible explanation that hurts even more than the fact of abandonment itself. Particularly when a man has managed to appear loving and affectionate practically to the moment of departure, even the simple statement, "I don't love you anymore," is bewildering. One woman said that while her husband was in the process of telling her that he was leaving, her eyes wandered over to the dining room table on which there was a vase containing the dozen roses that he had given her two days earlier, together with a card that professed his deep love for her.

It's exhausting to try to match up those disparate pieces of information—"He said he loved me yesterday and he's leaving me today." That way lies madness! And there's a reason for that madness. It comes about when the wife is subject to a form of emotional abuse called "gaslighting." The term refers to a 1944 Ingrid Bergman film, *Gaslight*, in which the devious husband of the trusting but delicate heroine secretly flickers the gaslights from the attic every evening. When his wife comments on the strange fluctuations, he tells her that she's imagining things. By purposefully loosening her grip on reality, he convinces her that she's going mad. In our context of WAS, gaslighting is defined as a manipulation by which, in an effort to rationalize leaving, a husband emphatically insists on a nonsensical explanation, which causes his wife to feel like she's losing her mind.

She becomes destabilized as her focus is deflected from what she's just learned her husband has been doing (the deception and affair) to what her husband is currently saying (the confusing justification). It is practically impossible in the moment of revelation for her to break the ingrained habit of trusting what her husband says and accept the possibility that he's lying and manipulating her for his own gain. The work of revising her vision of him will take long, hard months to achieve. So although what he's saying doesn't jibe with her perceived reality, she keeps trying to make it make sense and pound that round peg into a square hole—an impossible task.

Several runaway husbands who themselves participated in the study said they left because they weren't happy and hadn't been for a long time. They didn't really know why, but they just weren't enjoying their lives. Jed Diamond, the author of *The Irritable Male Syndrome*, describes the "flipping of a switch"—the emotional shift that leads some men to suddenly and dramatically exit their marriages. He says, "When a guy makes the decision that 'I don't want to be married any more,' often he has no real logical reason why. He just has a feeling and will say, 'I just knew I couldn't go on anymore. It was a wonderful marriage and the things I said in the all the cards were true. I did love her yesterday, but I woke up today and it was gone.'" Diamond explains further, "The human brain wants to have a reason. On the flip side of 'I've already decided to leave' is 'I have to have some reason.' It doesn't make sense to say, 'My life has been happy and I did love my wife, but I stopped.' You have to have a reason." Hence, the husband seizes on any reason, sensible or not, in the hope that his wife will buy it and let him move on.

Absence Makes the Heart Grow Colder

At some point during the twenty-three days when I was away on the book tour promoting *My Sister, My Self*, my husband was at home tidying his desk. The morning after I returned, Ingrid, who cleaned for us twice a month, asked me whether my husband was moving out. I laughed, "No, Ingrid, he's at work! Why would you say that?" She answered, "Vikki, I've been working for you for a long, long time and I've never seen his desk so clean!" Of course, Ingrid was right. That was the evening that my husband came home from work and hit me with the brutal news.

Before I started researching Wife Abandonment Syndrome, I wouldn't have given a second thought to the fact that my husband's departure coincided with my return home from my trip. However, after hearing repeatedly from SWAP participants that the revelation occurred after one or the other had been away, the correlation became undeniable: the majority of men announce their departure following a separation. The fact that the couple is apart helps a man who is contemplating leaving firm up his resolve. Regardless of whether it's a month-long trip or a short weekend get-away, somehow the remnants of the glue that kept the couple together dries out while they are apart.

Sometimes, the traveling is completely legitimate: "He took our son skiing in Aspen"; "He went to visit his brother in Memphis"; "My ex had signed up to take a distance education Master's Degree and went to Denver for the orientation"; "I was on a vacation with my daughter for two weeks"; "He wanted me to go to my mother's seventieth birthday in Halifax"; "I went, at his suggestion, to Guatemala to learn Spanish for my medical practice." But occasionally, something about the traveling smells a little fishy: "My husband went away for a 'weekend conference' (Yeah, right!)"; "He was going off to Berlin to do 'research' (but he was going to meet *her* there)."

Two things can happen to the husband who is thinking of leaving when the couple spends time apart. Either he experiences the relief of not having to fake an ill-fitting role any more or he has a chance to try out the reality of his future life with his girlfriend. Either way, a separation often acts as a dress rehearsal for the real thing.

The Cruelest Month

The analysis of the SWAP interviews unearthed another surprising statistic: a very high percentage of women in the study were left during the three months of November to January. Forty-four percent of the marriages ended during this time, peaking around the holidays—Thanksgiving, Christmas and New Year's. Several men left on New Year's Eve. One man walked out on Thanksgiving, his former wife recalling, "My turkey was in the oven and I was in the kitchen preparing an apple pie. I had a houseful of guests on the way. He waited until all the guests had arrived and made sure they saw him walk out the door."

Speculating on why that period of the year is the most vulnerable, one could imagine three factors. First, the husband feels the pressure of having to appear to be the happy host at holiday social events and just can't face it. Second, the husband's girlfriend doesn't want to endure yet another holiday while her boyfriend is celebrating with his family, so she puts pressure on him to make up his mind. A study participant suggested the third factor: "Maybe these men get the itch in the winter as part of a seasonal depression? Maybe simply the dreariness outside pushes them to look elsewhere for some, ahem, warmth?" Whatever the explanation, it does seem clear that the dead of winter contributes to the mortality of marriages.

CHAPTER 6

Catalog of Heartbreak

I've been there, so you'd think I wouldn't be shocked, but the words and images women in the study used to describe their first reaction to the revelation that the marriage was over blew me away. Normal descriptive words didn't begin to express it for them. Words like sad, distraught, devastated, hurt, bewildered, depressed—as evocative as they are in everyday conversation, they're just vanilla pudding compared with the intensity of the experience of having your life as you knew it blown up in the blink of an eye. It's as if, one minute, you're enjoying a relaxing family picnic on a cloud-free summer day. Ten minutes later, after the tornado has hit, you're dazed, battered and bleeding, your kids are traumatized and your life lies shattered in splinters on the ground around you. *And it was your beloved husband who sent the tornado your way!* I'm not kidding. It actually feels like that. One SWAP participant said, "Hearing what I heard, I felt like I'd been hit by a truck. This is an amazing thing—these metaphors—they're actually not metaphorical. This is how you feel—shattered—hit by a truck—stabbed in the heart. I really did feel I was hit by a Mack truck."

If you're squeamish, you may want to skip over the next few pages because the words the SWAP participants used to try to convey the depths of their anguish can only be described as raw. No, scratch that. It's important that you read it all or you won't get it—you won't understand the extent to which the women suffered. The following descriptions, which I call the **Catalog of Heartbreak,** are in answer to the question, "Do you remember what you thought and felt on hearing the news?"

- I felt intense physical pain. I remember my heart beating so hard I thought it was going to burst.
- I felt a really physical sense of being torn apart.
- Absolute shock and disbelief. In fact—I thought it was a movie rehearsal.
- I felt lost.
- It was like someone had stuck a knife into my stomach.
- I immediately got up and went into the bathroom and threw up.
- I felt as though a truck had hit me.
- My life was shattered.
- My eyes cried uncontrollably for a full day.
- I was in a pain fog for months. I hurt so much.
- HURT, HURT, HURT, anger, confusion, longing.
- I started feeling physical pain in my chest, which scared me, thinking that I might be having a heart attack (at 39).
- Heartache—I now know what that is and that heart pain really does exist.
- My heart dropped.
- If he had ripped my arm out, it wouldn't have hurt as much.
- The very first thing I felt on hearing the news? My heart break.
- I felt like someone had hit me in the stomach. I was physically ill and I could not believe my ears! I was absolutely traumatized. My whole body had horrible hives.
- I felt like I was above watching myself receive this awful news; that's how surreal it was.
- Despair firstly. Fear, doused with times of "out of body–like tolerance."
- I wanted my life to end right there.
- Devastation like none I had experienced before.
- Devastated, confused and just not understanding.

- I was completely devastated, horrified, disbelieving, felt like I was having a horrible nightmare that couldn't possibly be true, threw up, sobbed and had a surreal sensation the whole time—that it couldn't possibly be happening.
- It felt as if he took a large stick and slammed it into my stomach.
- The bottom fell out of my being.
- I felt crushed, steamrollered, and then I felt as if I was falling off a cliff.
- I felt like someone punched me in the gut.
- I had the image of a tube in my chest and that all my energy and capacity for love was draining out of me.
- I had something I never had before, a panic attack, where I totally fell apart and couldn't breathe.
- I felt like someone had stepped on my chest and emptied my lungs of air. It was horrible.
- I felt that I was watching my life being blown apart.
- My heart hurt, I thought I was going to throw up, I got nervous gut; I thought this couldn't be happening.
- I was heartbroken. I just can't describe the feeling. My heart broke.
- I felt as if I had been kicked in the stomach and in fact threw up several times that evening.
- I literally got dizzy and was STUNNED. Everything became foggy.
- I was shattered.
- I felt like he'd plunged a knife in my heart and every word he said turned it.
- I felt like going through the floor while a knife was in my heart; I felt paralyzed.
- Absolute shock and terror.
- I was stunned. I couldn't think. I felt physically and emotionally paralyzed. I retreated inside myself.
- My heart was broken. I just wanted to die.
- Shock, despair and utter disbelief.
- Traumatized and just raw hurt.

- I felt like someone had punched me in the stomach.
- I felt like I had stepped on a landmine. This was so out of the blue. I was in total shock.
- I felt like I was hit with a ton of bricks.
- I thought that I had lost all grip on reality. I felt as if I was thrashing around in a nightmare.
- I had a strange physical sensation—like my brain had been shot with a stun gun.
- I was very confused and numb.
- My whole world collapsed.
- Disbelief, shock, horror, sick, scared, disbelief!

Written on the Body

Heart break. Landmine. Nightmare. SWAP participants used vivid imagery in their efforts to express their reactions to an extraordinary experience. The metaphors fall into three categories: physical (heartbreak), violent (landmine) and surreal (nightmare). There's no doubt that every woman reacted physically to the news, and that the common thread was a terrible feeling of physical pain. If you're lucky enough not to have experienced anything like this, you may be surprised to learn that deep emotional pain is intensely physical and located in the body—usually in the chest or stomach. The brain is so powerful that even just hearing something shocking can throw your whole system into an uproar that can continue for months.

The violent imagery is another way of putting into words the feeling the women had of having been brutalized, if not physically then emotionally. Common themes were of being blown apart and feeling like a knife had been plunged into her body. Although a metaphor, to the woman herself, it actually *feels* real—hard to describe, but it does.

The third theme, the surreal quality (described in the subway vignette that introduced an earlier chapter), was reported by almost everyone to some extent. When her reality as she knew it has been suddenly obliterated, an abandoned wife slips into an altered state. In this state of shock, time becomes malleable, the body feels strange and the world becomes unfamiliar. She can't make sense of what she's hearing because she can't think straight—she's too numb to think at all. Her brain just can't handle it. She enters a dream state.

Trauma

The German word for dream is *traum*. A commonly accepted definition of psychological trauma is:

> a type of damage to the psyche that occurs as a result of a traumatic event. A traumatic event involves a singular experience or enduring event or events that completely overwhelm the individual's ability to cope or integrate the ideas and emotions involved with that experience. Trauma can be caused by a wide variety of events, but there are a few common aspects. It usually involves a complete feeling of helplessness in the face of a real or subjective threat to life, bodily integrity, or sanity. There is frequently a violation of the person's familiar ideas about the world, putting the person in a state of extreme confusion and insecurity. This is often seen when people or institutions depended on for survival violate or betray the person in some unforeseen way.

This definition talks about damage to the psyche caused when a person is unable to integrate a sudden change in his or her reality. It specifies that the person feels helpless in the face of a threat, and that trauma often occurs as a result of betrayal by someone on whom the person has depended. What could be a better description of Wife Abandonment Syndrome?

Additionally, scientists have now determined through brain scan technology that trauma actually changes the structure and function of the brain. J. Douglas Bremner, M.D., of Yale University's School of Medicine writes, "Recent studies indicate that extreme stress can cause measurable physical changes in the hippocampus and medial prefrontal cortex, two areas of the brain involved in memory and emotional response." So, as a result of the psychological trauma women experience when they are suddenly abandoned, they undergo undetectable but very real physical changes to the brain that lead to months or years of disturbance in their normal, pre-abandonment functioning.

It's surprising to note that none of the women reported their first reaction to be anger. The universal reactions were shock, devastation and disbelief. Not one said, "I'll kill him!" which, with the gender reversed, was the first response of some of the handful of abandoned husbands I heard from. Among the women, that rage initially was nowhere to be found. One wrote, "I *wish* I'd reacted with anger instead of trauma." The anger does come, but it comes later.

His Reaction to Her Reaction

While the women were suffering the torments of hell, what were the runaway husbands doing? Thirty-one percent left the very day of the revelation. Forty-three percent had cleared out by the next day, and 54 percent were gone within a week. But most startlingly, 13 percent had moved out *prior* to informing their wives that they were leaving!

The majority of the men fled directly to the welcoming arms of their girlfriends. Wives who were left behind often used the word "elated" to describe their husband's demeanor as he was packing up his things. But somewhere between the secret decision to leave and that breathless flight, those men changed. Men whom their wives had described as "easygoing," "solid," "predictable," "sensitive," "funny," "thoughtful," "logical and fair," "good-humored" and "Mr. Nice Guy" turned on them, like Dr. Jekyll metamorphosing into Mr. Hyde. Not only were they leaving, they were going to make damn sure that their wife knew every mistake she'd ever made, which they now insist drove them away.

Forty-five-year-old Kristen was devastated by her former husband's radical change in attitude: "I thought that we had a very good relationship and a very strong bond and that was certainly the message that my husband kept relaying to me—almost to the day he left." She was completely unprepared for what awaited her when that day came. "On the night he told me he wanted a divorce, his attack was vicious and violent—he didn't actually hit me, but there was a point at which I thought he might. He was banging his fists on the table and lifted it up and smashed it down. He accused me of so many things and some them went to the very core of me. Only he would know how to hurt me like that. I felt a lot of shame about that. That I failed him—failed the marriage."

The issue here is not that Kristen's husband doesn't have a right to be angry about things that happened in the marriage—no one is asserting that the wives being left are perfect. But he hadn't mentioned any of his complaints until that final conversation. She was confused and vulnerable when a case was made for her culpability, particularly because her husband seemed so sure and emphatic about it. In a typical statement, one SWAP participant said, "I bought it—it was all because I'd been so terrible. He had all the lists of all the ways I had not met his needs."

Paradoxically, it is the wives who often feel regret, whereas among the men, that sentiment is nowhere to be found. The women are heartsick in the face of all the things they have been told that they did wrong in the marriage, yet their husbands take no responsibility for the problems and express no remorse for the manner in which they leave.

I'm the Victim Here!

Men who left seemed to have to steel themselves in order to accomplish their vanishing act. Most refused to enter into a protracted discussion of the demise of their decades-long marriage—they just wanted to transmit the barest amount of information in the shortest amount of time and get out of there. Many wives said that they were confronted with a cold, hard stare as they begged for an explanation they could grasp. The departing husbands had to shut off any residual feelings because if they experienced empathy toward their distraught wives, their resolve might soften. Jed Diamond elaborates, "When they make the switch, they're so frightened that they're going to go back and be nice boys again that, in reaction to that, they become very rigid, 'No, I can't do that,' 'No, I won't do that,' 'No, I don't care if you're crying or weeping,' more out of their own fear of interacting, 'If I talk with her, if I listen to her, if I talk nicely to her, I'm going to want to come back and accommodate.' It is really their own inability to deal with conflict, their own inability to feel strong in themselves."

Shauna, 62 years old and married thirty-seven years, says she pleaded with her husband "to think of all the years we had spent together and all the problems we had overcome and the wonderful family we had raised. He looked at me like he couldn't stand me. And then he said he just didn't care one way or another how I felt. I had better get over it and get on with my life by myself."

The husband of 42-year-old Anne-Marie, married twenty-one years, invited her into the living room with their two teenaged daughters to economically inform the whole family at the same time that he no longer loved his wife. "He tells us that he has not been happy for a long time and he has the 'right' to be happy. And that was it! Both the kids and I are crying, and he is sitting cool as a cucumber on the opposite couch observing it all."

As the wives struggled to devise an explanation for the dramatic change that had made their husband unrecognizable, many settled on the same one—brain tumor. SWAP respondents clung to that account for their husband's actions like a shipwrecked sailor on a sinking raft. The same thought crossed my mind until I realized that a brain tumor would have killed him during his six-year affair! I seriously toyed with the possibility that he had been abducted by aliens who replaced him with a terrifically real replica—it sure seemed like that—but also discarded that explanation in the end. One thing was clear. I had no idea who this stranger was, but he seemed to have a wanton disregard for my feelings. Anything was possible, so to protect myself from the unpredictable behavior of this hologram that looked uncannily like my husband, I, like many other women in the study, removed the house key from my husband's key ring just before he left. That was the first indication to him that I wasn't going to continue being the accommodating wife I always had been, and that realization made him very mad.

I think my husband was stunned that I didn't see the validity of his decision and "get with the program." A couple of times during the first day or so after he left, he forlornly said, "I thought we could just sit at the dining room table and divide up our things and that would be that." But when he realized that I was not going to play by his rules, things turned ugly. Fleeing the house, he said, "I don't live here anymore so I don't have to pay a penny toward your expenses." Three times during the first week, as he came back and forth to pack up his things, he threatened, "You're going to be out on the street!" Later, he mystified me by asserting, "Everyone is going to see that *I'm the victim here!*" The last straw came months later. I had filed for divorce on the grounds of adultery and he responded by denying adultery (although admitting to a six-year affair—go figure). Then he counterfiled on the grounds of mental cruelty. That moment, when I read those two words on the papers from his lawyer, were among the worst in the whole ordeal.

Ann Patchet, the author of *Bel Canto*, writes, "A special kind of bewilderment comes of being wrongly accused," and over and over again, other women in the study also talked about being mystified. Fifty-four-year-old Kay recalls the moment when her husband, Jacob, made his shocking announcement of his intention to leave. "When I protested (it was as if he expected me to just automatically nod my head in agreement, shake hands with him and walk away), he turned on me—telling me that he had never, ever loved me, he couldn't remember one happy day during our thirty-four years together and that everything bad that had ever, ever happened to him was completely my fault."

Ellen, 67, contributed, "He seemed to have no capacity to understand what his behavior was doing to me and to our children and their families. I think he expected that it would all just pass as 'one of those things' and life would carry on much as before."

In the same vein, Dorothy, 59, wrote, "He had a very unrealistic picture of how I would receive this news and how it would change our lives. He thought that I would accept this, want what was best for him and remain friends. He thought that he would continue to be part of my social circle and was hurt when my friends snubbed him. He thought that I would remain in the matrimonial home and buy out his half; he suggested that I cash in my retirement savings to do this. He wanted me to accompany him to look for a new house for himself and his ladylove. Of course I said no."

Leading toward Healing

The events and emotions during the chaotic days and weeks following the revelation mark the first of the **Transformational Stages** of Wife Abandonment Syndrome—Tsunami. Although almost all women are in a state of shock, there are important steps that can be taken to help navigate past this shipwreck in life so it doesn't end with drowning. Here we draw on the first of the **Seven Steps for Moving Forward**: recognize that the chaos won't last forever. In a time of crisis, it's important not to make major decisions in your life. You need to recognize that you are not thinking properly and your job at the moment is just to survive—make it through the days until you can start to function again. One woman offered this bit of advice, "Just do the next thing." Don't think about the future beyond what your next task of the day is: "Oh, yes. It's 6 o'clock—now I must eat something for dinner." If you continue to just do the next thing, eventually you will find your way to solid ground.

I want to share with you a little trick that helped me escape my torturous thought spiral in the early days—jigsaw puzzles. When you've got too much dangerous time on your hands, you can eat up hours doing a thousand-piece puzzle. Rather than searching for meaning in your life, you can pass a whole evening searching for the man in the blue hat! Bingo! Soon you're exhausted and it's bedtime and you've made it through another day.

Another strategy is to remember that your mind plays tricks on you in the middle of the night. I always suggest to clients not to believe anything they think between midnight and 6 a.m. Thinking is distorted during those hours. Often, when you've spent the whole night agonizing about something, the issue seems insignificant in the cool light of morning.

Don't take risks! It is important to realize that your safety can sometimes be in jeopardy. You must be hyper-vigilant when you are cooking, crossing the street or driving a car. If you can't concentrate, don't drive! If you do drive, be very, very careful. I nearly had a fatal accident during the first week after my husband left. I've heard of others who also made stupid mistakes behind the wheel.

Now is the time to turn to friends and family and ask for help, especially if you have young children to care for. Keeping life as normal as possible for your children must be your first priority, and sometimes that means getting someone close to come over, make dinner and help them with homework. If at all possible, try not to fall apart in front of the kids too often. I know it's a lot to ask, but you will feel better about yourself later on if you can manage to defer the real misery until after their bedtime.

You can expect that you may do some crazy things (like throwing your husband's clothes out the window or telephoning him repeatedly in the middle of the night). Here you have to cut yourself some slack. In following chapters, you'll learn how you can get back into some semblance of control of your life. But remember; although you are feeling "crazy" now, it doesn't mean that you will always remain in this altered state! As my mother used to say (although you won't believe it while you're in the thick of it), "This too shall pass!"

Virginia's To-Do List

Virginia, 51, thought she was going insane when her high school sweetheart turned his back on her after thirty-one years of marriage. With three kids to look after, she didn't have the luxury of losing it, so instead, she made a simple little "to-do" list to keep herself off antidepressants:

1 I took vitamin supplements every day.
2 I went out every day, even if it was just to stand on the back step; sometimes it was to take a walk.
3 I exercised every day, sometimes only five minutes on the treadmill, but I did it.
4 I was not allowed to return to bed once I got out of it in the morning.
5 I forced myself to eat six times a day; sometimes it was just a spoonful of yogurt.
6 When the panic would come, I had friends to call.

I wrote these six things on a paper and would check them off as I accomplished each one every day. I know that sounds flaky, but it really did help, and that was the focus of my day sometimes. Eventually, I gained strength.

CHAPTER 7

Uproar!

It was a Saturday, three weeks after he left, 5 p.m. or so. I'd bought some chicken soup, which I heated up and ate. I was in a lot of pain and there was an endless night ahead of me until I could finally go to bed around 10. I decided that I wouldn't telephone anyone or do anything—that I'd just stay with what I was feeling and not push it away. I poured myself a glass of wine and sat at the dining room table in front of the jigsaw puzzle I'd bought (putting the pieces back of my life back together again?). The ticking of the clock was the only sound in the otherwise silent room. The pain was almost unbearable, but I knew it wouldn't kill me. It was a pure feeling and felt right. After twenty-one years, I needed to feel it. Soon after I let it come, it started to recede. I decided that I would welcome the pain over the coming months—it meant that, for me at least, the marriage had meaning.

If you've been there, you know exactly what I'm talking about. Emotional pain of this magnitude is physical—you *actually* feel it inside. It makes breathing hard, moving is an effort; your mind is in lock-down. For me, it was accompanied by nausea that dogged me unrelenting for months.

Carolina, 42, was filled with optimism when she moved to San Diego from her native Chile to get married, but seven years later, following her husband's unexpected departure, that buoyant excitement was replaced by fear, shame and a sense of desolation.

The first few months, I totally isolated myself from every-
body. Friends would come around, banging on the door—I
refused to leave the house. I would go to the supermarket
at night when I knew I wouldn't bump into anybody. I
wouldn't speak to people on the phone. I lost a lot of
weight—55 lbs. There were times when I wanted to go
to sleep and never wake up. I never actually thought about
killing myself—I just didn't want to go on—it was like I
didn't exist.

I'd become dependent on him financially and felt desperate about money, panicked about my status in the country—
was it going to be affected by divorce? I was terrified about
losing my home. I'd spent two years renovating this home
to raise a family in it. We were going to adopt children. In
the summer, we had discussed it. It was definitely going to
happen!

I had given up my career, I had given up my dreams and
a lot of my ambitions to be here for him and this is the outcome—a terrible sense of failure.

Carolina's story illustrates the typical state of mind during the
first part of this **Transformational Stage**—Tornado. You're reeling
from how dramatically your life has changed. Your thoughts are
spinning wildly as you try to come up with some desperate plan
to make this not be happening or at least to understand it. Your
feet are not on the ground, and you grasp wildly at anything that
will help you feel more stable.

You have no idea what the future will bring and may wonder
if there's any hope of reconciliation—perhaps it was a midlife crisis or temporary insanity on his part! Is it fixable? Where will you
live, what will you do for work, how will you sort out the legal
aspects with him and where will that leave you? Your previously
well-defined future is now shrouded in fog.

With your emotions out of control, you'll probably do things
that won't make you very proud, looking back on them later.
Desperate to escape the wretched feeling inside, you'll try any-

thing to lessen the pain, sometimes getting yourself into trouble. You may drink or smoke too much, misuse drugs, obsessively seek information about your ex and his girlfriend, wear out your friends and even find yourself in the arms of a man you have no business dating.

You're in the process of redefining your reality but it's awfully hard to keep all the differing versions straight in your head at one time. That confusion makes you vulnerable to accepting your husband's definition of the story. You may be comforted, however, by learning that it's normal that you are seesawing between two simultaneous conflicting emotional realities. The first is defined by your default experience of your husband—one that you took as a "given" perhaps for decades—your view of him as a loving caring man. This hard-wired internal reality tells you that he is trustworthy and you can depend on what he says as being valid and meaningful.

It co-exists, however, with evidence to the contrary because he actually betrayed you, lied to you and took advantage of your trusting nature. This internal reality tells you to watch out, be careful and not expect anything good or kind to come in your direction from your husband. These two opposing realities flicker back and forth in your heart and mind like a religious picture in a storefront window that jumps from one scene to the next when you shift your head. Both realities fight for dominance; your heart keeps slipping back longingly to the version of the man who gave you his love, while your mind struggles to redefine him as the self-involved stranger who treated you without respect.

Once this period of extreme instability ends, you move into the Thunderstorm Stage. Here you feel besieged, raw and fearful and don't know when the next thunderbolt will strike. Your emotions ricochet wildly from anger (lightning), to grief (rain), to fear (wind). Although you may be back into your day-to-day routine, you're just hanging on, vulnerable to any little thing that could tip you back to that state of total chaos.

By the end of the Thunderstorm Stage, you'll probably be in the midst of the legal process that defines your future reality. You will most likely have clarified some of the details, such as whether you can afford to stay where you are living or if you'll need to find work if you're not currently employed. And you'll be taking the first shaky baby steps toward your new identity as a single person. For some of you, like me, this may be the first time in your life that you are living alone. And, as you come out of the storm, you'll have achieved at least a bit more control over your emotions. You won't feel like you're in the middle of an emergency *all* the time.

It's all normal. This craziness is normal. We'll now explore what a woman goes through in the months following the revelation of WAS. We'll talk about the pain, the endless obsessing, revenge fantasies, the crazy things we do, the longing and heartaching wish that if you could just have the "old" him back for an hour to listen to all you have to say, he would understand and come to his senses.

The Gift of a Musical Heart

If you are in the first months following WAS, I'm sure that you're exhausted and feel emotionally defenseless. All your energy is spent in a struggle to keep going, leaving little remaining to maintain the stimulus barrier that typically serves as a buffer between you and the world around you. That makes it hard to protect yourself from further hurt, but it also makes gestures of kindness more profoundly felt. A smile from a stranger at a street corner will fill your eyes with tears and give you the courage to push through the next hour of your difficult day. A wordless squeeze on your shoulder when you pass a colleague in the corridor boosts your spirits just when you really need it. My neighbors gave me a gift of a shiny silver heart-shaped paperweight that lies in the palm of my hand like a heavy flat stone. When you shake it, it makes a musical clang. I left it in the middle of the kitchen table and picked it up to give it a shake every time I passed. It was weird how that clanging chime always managed to make me feel so much better.

Shortly after my husband left, my daughter offered to put some of her music on my iPod to inspire me on the treadmill at the gym. As soon as I heard Christina Aguilera's song "Fighter," I knew that it would became the anthem of my recovery. In the song, a woman is telling the man who betrayed her that instead of resenting him, she wants to thank him. She says that, rather than bringing her down, all the suffering he put her through made her stronger, made her work harder and made her wiser. The refrain in the song is, "Thanks for making me a fight-er!"

During that painful first year, if you'd seen me running hard on the treadmill, you might have wondered what that crazy woman was doing, hunched over and jabbing the air from time to time with a "one-two" punch. Had you been plugged into my iPod, you'd know the jab coincided with every time the song got to the word "fight-er." That song spurred me on to be tougher, made my skin thicker and helped me be smarter in dealing with things. I'd never before thought of myself as a fighter, but the song strengthened my resolve to stand up for what was right, not only for myself, but also for all the other women who'd been so unjustly hurt.

As part of the study, I asked SWAP participants what music helped them and received a long list of songs to cry by, songs that soothed, and songs that made them feel stronger, even defiant (the list is in the back of the book, but, as you can imagine, the hands-down favorite was Gloria Gaynor's, "I Will Survive").

One night I decided to post a list of the theme songs on the Runaway Husbands website. Before doing so, I wanted to listen to the 30-second fragments of each of them that are available on-line. One after the other, the songs told of suffering in a way that was far more evocative than mere words could convey. I imagined each woman listening to her special song and finding either solace or a release for her pain.

Immersing myself in the music was a deep emotional experience for me, and when I'd listened to them all, I played the full version of one of *my* songs, "Landslide," sung by the Dixie Chicks. I cried my heart out for the first time in over a year. What got to me was thinking about all the love I'd poured into my relationship, how I'd loved loving my husband, and what a waste it was to give so much to someone who was incapable of valuing it.

A number of SWAP participants, however, said they couldn't listen to music at all—it hurt too much. A song would come on the loudspeaker at the mall and next thing they knew, they'd be sobbing silently into a wad of soggy tissues in the end stall of the ladies' room. One woman explained why she avoided music at all costs: "There were too many songs that reminded me of certain memories, or the words themselves were too painful." Another woman wrote, however, that now she's into country music for the first time in her life because she can sing along really loud and it makes her smile!

Following trauma, the perilously thin state of that stimulus barrier means that the wife who has been left will be unable to protect herself from reacting to the myriad cues or triggers that litter her landscape. Even after she has purged every shred of her former husband's clothing and personal belongings from their joint domicile, reminders will keep cropping up. A glimpse of his handwriting in an inscription in a book will be enough to set her stomach churning. Running across old photos, receiving mail for him after the forwarding has lapsed, finding that he's still listed as her spouse when she goes to renew her library card or passport— these simple little things will continue to pack a punch for a long time that can ruin her whole day. In the months immediately after the revelation, however, they can set her back a whole week!

No Way 'Round It

The other evening I was walking my little dog, Chloe, when I came upon a Boston terrier running all alone down the sidewalk. I tied Chloe up to a fence, planning to rescue the frightened creature, when suddenly a pack of four or five dogs came barrelling around the corner. Two of them, a pit bull and a rottweiler, went for my terrified tethered puppy, who was screeching and jerking wildly trying to get away. Their owner came running, grabbed his dogs and, with great effort, threw them off mine. He managed to get them under control and corralled them up the stairs to his apartment. Miraculously, Chloe was not bitten.

But she's a changed little soul. Spunky, fearless Chloe is now much more cautious around other dogs, and you'd better believe that when we go for our evening walk, she pours all of her thirteen pounds of muscle into stopping me from getting anywhere near the place where the attack happened.

It's human (canine?) nature to try to avoid things that hurt. In abandonment, the pain comes partially from the outside (caused by the words and actions of your former spouse and erstwhile friends and family), but the really brutal assault is usually internal, fueled by relentless thoughts and powerful feelings that are hard to manage. Try as you might to control or banish them, they're stronger than you are and they win out in the end, at least in the short run.

Bonnie, married twenty-eight years, tried valiantly to suppress that pain but learned that it helped when she confronted it:

> I kept most of it in and every now and then, I'd let somebody see, just a few people, two friends. My sister saw my pain. I had a therapist at the time and let some out there, too. But I probably internalized most of it. Eventually I learned to cry—I wailed at times. If I was alone in the house and went to that deep place, I did let it out. I guess learning to wail helped.

Anita, married four years, found comfort in the belief that she wouldn't always feel so bad and devised a clever trick to help her remember that time would heal:

> Initially, after he removed his things, I talked myself into getting a hold of the idea that what I was feeling was only temporary; all things will pass. So, I made a 12" x 18" sign that said "temporary." No matter what I was doing in the house,

laundry, dishes, cleaning, etc., I would take that sign with me and place it where I could clearly see it. I found comfort in the word "temporary," expecting that if I read the word enough, I just might shake this god-awful anxiety in a month or two. Twelve months later, I had discontinued carrying it with me from room-to-room because I'd made signs that were permanently placed in every room in the house!

Of course we want the suffering to stop. But often the effort to circumvent it is exhausting and paradoxically more likely to delay healing than if we had just allowed ourselves to feel the full extent of it. The grief that follows such a profound loss is a necessary process, and, as the saying goes, there's no way around it—you have to go through it. But it's counterintuitive. You may worry that if you permit yourself to really feel it, you'll fall into a black hole and never recover, but the opposite is true. Constantly pushing it away keeps it lurking around just beyond the perimeters of your consciousness. When you face it, like I did that silent fall night seated in front of the jigsaw puzzle, the emotion has a natural point of resolution—you feel it fully, you suffer, and slowly, little by little, the intensity starts to soften.

Thirty-eight-year-old Jane, an architect from Tucson, did just that and found it opened her heart:

The way I dealt with it and this was not conscious—was simply by sinking into the pain. It hurt like hell but I think it saved me. I always thought of myself as capable and independent, but the pain was so bad, and not being able to fix things was so obvious and great, I was sort of stripped naked. That sense of being completely and utterly vulnerable stripped away my defenses and allowed me to feel all the love coming in. It's almost as though when the walls came down, the pain flooded in but so did the love. And there was something cleansing about how searing the pain was.

Thomas Moore wrote in *Dark Night of the Soul* about the value of immersing yourself in your feelings:

> You can thin your life effectively by taking the lead of your dark night. Go with developments, rather than against them. If you feel lost, be lost in ways that suit you and make you feel like a participant in your life. If you feel empty, empty out your life where it needs it. If you feel sad, let sadness be your dominant feeling. Being in tune with your deep mood is a way of clarifying yourself. Speak for it. Show it. Honor it.

Moore goes on to address the potential of grief for renewal. But he also warns against making your suffering into your identity:

> Temporary insanities, like those of hard loss and grief, are always potentially creative, depending on how you deal with them. The temptation always is to sink too far into self-pity and to find relief in the compassion of others. It's important to feel the sadness, but emotion is always only a partial resolution. Grief is complete only with a shift in being, in the way you live, think, and relate to the world.

Susan Anderson, the author of *The Journey from Abandonment to Healing*, also writes about the need to immerse yourself in your feelings. Anderson, who was herself abandoned in the midst of what she perceived to be "a loving, successful, twenty-year relationship," labels this part of the recovery process "shattering" and encourages those suffering to enter into it deeply. She writes:

> The secret is to get into the moment and stay there as often as possible. This allows you to work with the energy rather than against it, to experience this time of stark and naked

separateness for all that it's worth. In the moment, you experience the intensity of life as a separate human being.

I agree with Moore and Anderson wholeheartedly, with one caveat—you must couple this embracing of the pain with a genuine wish to rebuild your life or else you risk making the abandonment into a badge of honor that defines you. Although you may genuinely have been a victim of your former husband's callousness, you must not turn that into a tattoo you wear for a lifetime. It's important not to develop a victim mentality just because you have been victimized.

A victim mentality means that throughout your life you focus on the wrongs done to you, and this narrative of your injured self serves to garner sympathy and support from others. By definition, it means that you believe you are powerless to improve your future. And I know you are not powerless, no matter what has happened in your past or how rough things are at the moment. So, yes, you can say you were victimized … but no! Don't let that become your identity.

In the early months, it will probably be close to impossible to be able to glimpse the invaluable potential for improving your life imbedded in all that you are going through. But it's there! We'll hear more about how women turned poison into medicine in future chapters. But first, you have to get through the crazy time.

CHAPTER 8

Crazy Time

Ah women! I asked the same question to both men and women who had been left—what was the craziest thing you did during the Tornado and Thunderstorm stages? One man wrote that when he came home to an emptied house and realized his departed wife was driving to her parents' home in another state, he took a plane there to precede her, broke into his in-laws' home and sat in the living room with a shotgun across his lap waiting for his wife and her parents to arrive. Fortunately, he got bored while he was waiting and telephoned a friend, who begged him to get the hell out of there. He left before his wife arrived.

I'm not implying that all the abandoned men in the study reported such a violent response, but the fact is that one did, and not one of the women went anywhere near there. And the women ... try as they might to make an impressive statement, their actions were by and large purely symbolic. One woman broke her husband's collection of 45 rpm records; another ripped his leather jacket to shreds; another doused a couple of his books in perfume; and a really "evil" woman said she cleaned the bathroom sink with his toothbrush while they were still living together and spit in his tea (just the sink?). One admitted that the craziest thing she did was to buy a $300 food processor with all the attachments. She said that it was pretty but ridiculous because she doesn't enjoy

cooking all that much. And finally, another woman, trying dili-
gently to answer my query about the crazy things she did, said, "I
did something different with my hair today—does that count?"

Fifty-four-year-old Monica, although she was frantic at the
time, now laughs when she remembers her crazy state of mind
one night a few days after her accountant husband of twenty-six
years moved in with a secretary from his office:

> Something happened to me that night. I convinced myself
> that he really wanted to come back and started to fantasize
> that he would come to his senses. So I wrote him an email
> begging him to return and sent it at 1 a.m.
>
> My thinking was altered and I spent the rest of the night
> in a fever of anticipation at his response. I imagined that
> he would rush to call me the next morning when he got the
> email at work and I would ask him to drop home on his way
> to his girlfriend's apartment. I thought I would become a
> sex-goddess and give him sex any way he wanted. I hatched
> all sorts of fantastic plans—like opening the door in a rain-
> coat, push-up bra and panties, the house warm and inviting
> with scented candles.
>
> Then I thought, why wait? I would show up at his office
> with a beach bag in which I'd have a blanket, incense and a
> can of whipped cream. We'd make love on the vinyl tile floor
> next to the fish tank under the fluorescents! (I said, I wasn't
> thinking normally.) I was totally turned on, imaging our
> x-rated reunion.

In the light of dawn, with no response from her husband,
Monica's x-rated anticipation fizzled into despair.

Several women wrote that they acted out their grief in overtly
self-destructive ways. Cassie, married eighteen years, reported that
she locked herself in her room for three days. "I would get up
long enough to smoke and take a Xanax and go back to sleep."
Brooke, trying to survive the loss of her husband of twelve years,
said that she "spent about 36 hours watching T.V. without sleep,

stuffing my face with every single piece of garbage I could possible fit into it—just so I could feel numb."

A number of women sought out the arms of virtual strangers in order to make it through the night, an act of desperation which one described as "moral collapse." Trying to soothe the hurt and prove that they were still desirable, they behaved in atypical ways that inevitably brought them a sense of shame when the chaos subsided.

I would wager a guess that thoughts of suicide flickered across the minds of most, if not all, SWAP participants at some point, even in the form of the passive wish that Carolina wrote about that she just wouldn't wake up tomorrow. But the most painful stories were from women who were unable to tolerate it all and were close to acting on those thoughts. Here's a glimpse at the darkest hours of some desperate ex-wives:

- Pina wrote: "One night I actually contemplated going to a beach and simply walking into the water. It was brief and I knew deep inside that I wouldn't. But I was at a point where I questioned why on earth I'd want to go on living when the thing I had valued most had been thrown back in my face as if it was worthless by the very person who I felt should have cared."
- Maude contributed: "Once the kids had moved out, I actually bought a hose, planning to die in the garage. I did start it but didn't follow through on it because suddenly it dawned on me that he would probably actually appreciate it if I did commit suicide."
- Vivian, who quickly came to her senses, now describes the suicide attempt as the craziest thing she did during this period: "He was soooo not worth it. One night I sat in my car with the engine running and the garage door closed. I just couldn't face my life alone."
- Jeanine "booked a trip to Amsterdam, to sign myself into an assisted suicide clinic. I canceled, then rebooked, then canceled again."

- Finally, Rose was saved by a special kind of love: "If it had-n't been for my dogs, who need me and love me uncon-di-tionally, I would have killed myself. They are the only reason I'm still alive today."

As you spin around in the Tornado Stage, you're buffeted by two opposing forces. On the one hand, part of you has a strong need to block your former husband out of your life in order to protect yourself from learning, hearing, or seeing anything that can re-injure you. It's this impulse that has you jumping to turn off the radio when "your song" comes on and steering clear of restaurants and stores you used to frequent together for fear you might run into him (and her).

On the other hand, you're desperate for information. You're driven to gain some mastery over all the chaos and believe you won't be able to rest until you know absolutely everything that was going on when you were married. Against your better judgment, you feel compelled *ad nauseum* to delve into the areas of your husband's current life that are guaranteed to drive you bonkers.

You may find yourself doing a lot of sneaking around, driving past the shuttered windows of your ex's girlfriend's house, trying to hack into his phone messages, track his credit card bills or send off ill-advised emails which would only confirm his belief that his wife was a nut! Here's a sampling of the obsessive acts of some SWAP participants:

- "For weeks, I would check his voicemail at home and at work (I knew his passwords), to somehow feel connected to him again. I acted like a detective to get some more answers about who he really is. Three weeks after I moved, I heard a voicemail from a woman I didn't know, saying 'I'll see you later at your house, babe.' Ouch!"
- "One morning, a few months after he had left, I went to the house where he was staying with his girlfriend. I waited in my car with the windows open. I smelled their coffee and

heard their radio. I guess I thought that I would confront them when they came out to leave for work. I remember looking at my watch and saying to myself, 'If they're not out by 8:30 a.m., I'll leave.' I don't know why or what I thought I was doing. I had an overwhelming need to see where he was. Looking back, I'm glad I didn't wait around. I cried all the way home—had to pull over a couple of times off the road."

- "I photocopied emails he wrote to 'the other woman' and sent them to his family to prove he was the liar and I wasn't insane."
- "I hired a private investigator to follow him and the other woman."

Don't Press Send ...

Email—an ever so tempting medium of immediate gratification, which often leads to lingering regret. How many times did you get up in the middle of the night with the absolute conviction that you must tell your husband one essential thing right that minute? If not sooner! If only he knew this, either he'd feel enormous regret for his actions or perhaps, if you're lucky, he'd feel a crumb of the hurt he made you feel. But if he were vulnerable to feeling hurt by your accusations, he wouldn't be the kind of man who could run away with no regard for your feelings. He has his armor up, and your attacks only make you look desperate and pathetic—and you know that. And because you *never* get the satisfaction you crave from having sent the message, you end up re-injuring *yourself* instead of making a dent in him.

When I was in the Tornado Stage and so buffeted by emotion that I couldn't think straight, I was lucky to have the counsel of my two sensible adult daughters. They were also reeling from the revelation of their stepfather, but were slightly removed from the intensity of the storm. At one point, I emailed my older daughter about my wish to send a cyber-attack. Here is her sage advice:

Don't send that email. Please. Just don't. PLEASE!!!!!!!! I
think you have to let it go. YOU know the things you wrote
are true and everyone else does, too. But, I'm certain that
he will never see things that way. He has a million and one
excuses and justifications in his mind, none of which are of
concern to you. You're trying to negotiate with a man that
doesn't exist anymore.

Ask yourself, what do you expect to happen if you send
that email? What will you feel? How will you affect things?
What are you wishing will happen? Are those hopes or
desires realistic, or do they even reflect what you really feel
and want? Please don't send that email. It's in NO WAY
constructive. Besides, he doesn't deserve that much of you.

My grateful response to her was:

O.K. Just wanted to hurt him. I suppose I have to stop
caring. You're right. Thanks! Sorry to involve you but I
appreciate your unerring wisdom.

To which she responded:

To be honest, I think the email probably wouldn't hurt him
so much as make him more angry at you, and see you as
"hysterical," "irrational," etc. It would just make him dis-
miss you more. I was thinking that this stuff that you're
wrestling with, that we've all wrestled with in the face of a
break-up, is almost like an addiction: sending the emails,
leaving the hysterical phone messages, etc. It's like, we know
it's bad for us, that it won't solve the underlying problem or
give us any long term relief or happiness, but we need that
fix! And the pull to do those things is so strong. Maybe if
you approach it with that mentality, that it's like a drink
for an alcoholic, it might be easier to resist.

She hit the nail on the head. It *is* like an addiction, a fix. You
know it's not good for you in the long run but you can't resist

because it relieves some built-up stress momentarily. At first, when your emotions are in a perpetual uproar, you may not be able to hold yourself back, but as time goes on and you gain more control, you'll accept the fact that it is counterproductive and learn how to stop yourself.

My younger daughter, meanwhile, came up with a trick to help me avoid the urge to press "send." She said I should harness the email impulse by writing down everything I wanted to tell him, but instead of sending it, save it as a draft. I could send a grand summation blast when all this was over, if I was still so disposed. I found her suggestion helped because it felt good to write it all down—it did relieve some pressure—but it was smart not to send anything while I was still in the midst of the emotional turmoil. And, of course, by the time things were over, the urge to send the emails had passed and I was glad that I hadn't done so earlier.

As a result of this outpouring of familial sagacity, I came up with a rule of thumb—*DON'T PRESS "SEND" WHILE YOU'RE STILL IN YOUR PYJAMAS!* That means, don't send anything at all between the hours of midnight and 6 a.m., when your thinking is distorted, and hold off sending things between the daytime hours of 6 a.m. and midnight until you've thought it through. Twice. At least!

Revenge

One of the hardest things to take for most women is the realization that their former husband just fundamentally doesn't care anymore. The lack of remorse or even a "glance in my direction" mid-flight from a man who only days earlier had professed his deep and abiding love is often the cruellest cut of all. Many men are elated at the prospect of starting life anew with their affair partner, and the boring old wife seems to recede shockingly rapidly into a vague memory ("someone I once knew"?).

That dichotomy between a wife's post-separation experience and that of her husband was made crystal clear to me a few years ago when I was doing co-parenting counselling. The couple had separated a few weeks earlier and due to the high level of tension between them, I decided to initially meet with each of them individually. I met with the wife first and she spent the session tearfully agonizing about what had happened in the marriage. She tried to pry open her husband's head to understand his motivation, and sifted through every word he'd uttered for clues to how this happened, desperate to find a way to reverse the process.

Two days later, when I met with the husband, it was a totally different story. He used the session to talk about whether he should remain at his sister's home or rent an apartment, and wanted to discuss why his teenaged son hadn't told his friends about the separation. He barely mentioned his wife, with whom he'd shared a bed only a few weeks earlier. Although he wished her no harm, he was certainly not staying up nights worrying about how she was doing. And this was not a case of WAS, and the husband was not having an affair.

Ask yourself what percentage of your time you're willing to donate to a person who's probably not even thinking about you. As you're home obsessing about him, he's off having a glass of wine with a nice dinner. I love this quote from the Coen brothers' movie *No Country for Old Men*. In a pivotal scene, the semi-paralyzed retired sheriff is informed that the criminal who'd shot him and put him in a wheelchair had died in prison. He was asked whether it made him feel better to hear that the guy was finally dead. He responded, "All the time you spend trying to get back what's been took from ya, more is going out the door. After a while, you just try to get a tourniquet on it." In other words, you're wasting valuable energy because the only one that gets hurt by trying to exact revenge is you.

Vivian, who sounds phenomenally sensible, told why she answered "no" to the question in the study as to whether she had thought of or actually done anything to exact revenge:

There is a part of me that would like him to suffer some consequences for what he has done and it angers me that I don't think he ever will. But no, although I would like to hurt him,

I don't think anything I do will cause him any pain. He has no emotions, no feelings for me, so I doubt there would be any reaction that would give me any satisfaction. He is so closed to me, he would never allow himself to feel any pain from this. He is very good at protecting himself from being vulnerable.

But many women were not able to maintain such a calm assessment of the futile nature of acts of revenge. During the Tornado Stage, they were slightly unhinged and desperate to get the man's attention, even if just for a moment of guilty pleasure. But the only path available to most of the women to make any impression on their former husband was through fantasies of acts of revenge. It may have been cold comfort, but merely thinking of ways to even the score did help many women soothe their battered souls. Imagination is powerful and can go a long way toward helping the dreamer feel less helpless.

Shakespeare's claim that "hell hath no fury like a woman scorned" is illustrated by the violent imagery of some SWAP participants who really sunk their teeth into their answers to the question about revenge. Even I was startled by some of the colorful descriptions of fantasy retribution:

- "I had this BIZARRE fantasy, which I never told anyone about. It was a recurring dream. In the 'dream,' I carved the word 'ASSHOLE' into his forehead with a box cutter, so the scar remained forever. Now, I'm the least violent person around and I don't use the word 'ASSHOLE' in my normal vocabulary!"
- "I had a large knife from Nepal and imagined gouging his eyes out with it, but a friend told me I'd have to wear an orange prison suit and the color is awful on me!"
- "I had a recurring fantasy to roast him over an open campfire. However, every time I thought of this, I saw him with the same pasted-on smile that he always wore, even while he went round and round on the skewer."

- "I have fantasies of revenge all the time. Some of them are vicious, some of them are hilarious. I'd love to strip him naked, cover his skin in dimes secured with Crazy-Glue, and dump his sorry ass at the corner of Yonge and Bloor (prime panhandling territory in Toronto). My second choice would be to anchor a hot-air balloon in the parkette alongside his place and rig it to drop copies of his 'Us' email during daylight hours until the end of time. My third choice would be to forward every single one of the moronic emails he and the 'other' exchanged to all 600+ in his electronic address-book. My fourth choice would be ..."

- "One of the ways I used to get to sleep was to fantasize about how I would plan his killing. Would I do it myself? You can't hire somebody; it's too risky. Would I take a bus? Would I fly? How would I set it up? Where would I get the money? And it was very therapeutic to me, just to act it out in my head. My mother and I used to laugh that if he died before the divorce, we'd dress him up like a transvestite in a blue coffin—ha-ha-ha! Just to speak about it in a way that made us feel a little bit empowered for that ten minutes helped."

As colorful as the fantasies were, the real acts of revenge were relatively restrained. The spurned wives realized that the men who left were impervious to hurt from them directly, so most actual attempts at restitution were in the form of some kind of public humiliation—what one woman described as "calling in social currency." They ranged from making sure that all friends and family knew the real story of the affair, to notifying supervisors at work that the man was behaving unethically.

Sixty-seven-year-old Ellen, married twenty-eight years, emailed all the members of her husband's Rotary Club. She told them that he had lived a double life for two years, having had an affair with a married mother of two young children. He arrived at the next meeting, not knowing that everyone knew the truth, and was challenged when he attempted to give the "we drifted apart—it's so sad" routine. She got tremendous support from the members of the club and he stopped attending.

Sylvie, married thirty-five years, whose husband's girlfriend was one of his Ph.D. students, stumbled across a forty-page template he'd written to help her complete her thesis. Sylvie wrote, "He emailed her that he had written it 'in your voice' and he asked her to 'please keep this between the two of us.' She wrote back 'overjoyed' that the wretched Ph.D. would be FINISHED with the great 'template.'" Once the divorce was complete, Sylvie bundled all the evidence together and sent one copy to the girlfriend's supervisor and the other to the department head, which resulted in a formal investigation into academic fraud.

Some women reported that they had to resort to hopes of *Schadenfreude*, the elegant German expression that means "pleasure at someone else's misfortune," to get some comfort. Feeling helpless to make the slightest dent in her ex-husband's sense of well being, Veronica wrote that she pasted a banner to her computer that said, "Nothing I can say or do will hurt him—I'll just have to wait for life to do the job for me!" Reading it over every time she sat at her desk helped somewhat to dampen her overwhelming frustration. Ten months after her ex moved out, she was delighted to learn that he'd been dumped by his girlfriend.

The saying, "Living well is the best revenge," proves to be the healthiest sentiment of all. It helps struggling women turn away from measuring how their ex is faring to concentrating on the task of building their own lives. Imagination is powerful, and if you can start to envision a wonderful new life for yourself, you're halfway there! Once you can wrench your focus from all the miserable events of the recent past with *him* to your potential for achievement in your own future, you're well on your way to healing.

CHAPTER 9

Danger Zones

Journal entry: I nearly got killed today. I thought I was feeling pretty good, but I must really be dazed. I drove right past a stop sign into the stream of traffic onto St. Joseph Boulevard and then froze in the middle of the road. I just sat there, looking out my side window at the cars coming straight at me. I was stunned and unable to think. They screeched to a halt a few feet short of my door. I was lucky. No one hit me and there was no pile-up of other cars. Freaked me out. Then, today, I left the keys in the lock outside the front door to my house. Things I never ever do.

That traffic incident, three weeks after my husband left, made me aware of the fact that I was not thinking properly and alerted me to the fact that my life was in a danger zone. As a result, I became extra careful about driving consciously and deliberately, stopping fully at cross-streets and double-checking before proceeding. One woman I met said that while she was in that exhausted, stunned state, she actually did get into a horrible accident and totaled her car. She was lucky to walk away. I think that in some cases women just stop caring, which leads them to be less vigilant about protecting themselves.

A second subconscious indicator of the loosening of the self-protective instinct in reaction to WAS is weight loss. Almost every woman in the study reported losing a dramatic amount of weight—from five to fifty-five pounds—which is further proof of the traumatic nature of the event. For months, I didn't want to eat at all. It took tremendous effort to chew and swallow food that was completely unappealing and tasteless. By the time I stopped losing weight, I looked like a scarecrow, and my friends and family were anxiously encouraging me—*eat!*

Here are a couple of other women's thoughts on this:

- "During those early months, I was losing weight too fast; even a cup of coffee filled me up to the point of being uncomfortable."
- "I felt that I had fallen into another universe—I was totally disoriented—and, because I had been told something I could not swallow, I literally lost all interest in eating."

A third way that women are in a danger zone during this period relates to the fact that their husband's disregard for their safety has put them at risk for sexually transmitted diseases. It was a huge blow when the thought dawned on me that I needed to be tested for STDs. I had been having unprotected sex with a man who was having sex with a stranger who may also have been having sex with god knows who. I had married my husband in the mid-eighties, prior to concerns about HIV infection and always felt so secure that I never *ever* had to worry. I had literally trusted him with my life. It was with a heavy heart when I met with the public health nurse to be counseled the day I had to be tested.

Other women told of similar experiences:

- "He had been having unprotected sex for three years while still making love to me in that time. I told him that I did not appreciate him risking my life to HIV and other sexually transmitted diseases. He stated that he was 97 percent certain she was disease free. I went to the doctor and had all the tests run—I felt so abused."
- An email to an ex-husband: "For the past five (or more?) years, I have unknowingly been having unprotected sex through you with strangers and all their sexual partners. You put me at risk for HIV and AIDS, chlamydia, syphilis,

gonorrhoea, herpes, genital warts and all the rest, when I trustingly believed myself to be 100 percent safe. This is huge. How dare you take it upon yourself to risk my life!"

Many women in the study said that having their health and life jeopardized by the very person they believed would always protect them was a betrayal on the most primitive level possible. As already noted, for those who had been victims of childhood sexual abuse and had previously been unable to protect themselves, the damage to their sense of basic trust is incalculable.

Accepting the Unthinkable

We learned earlier that two of the **Seven Steps for Moving Forward** must be accomplished before you can move on from the Tsunami and Thunderstorm stages. The first is Step 2: "Accept that the marriage really is over." That's a tough one but a building block for what lies ahead. The wife often gets stuck in the rut of struggling to understand how things could have changed so radically and assessing if there is anything she can do to influence the turn of events. That requires deep thinking about what compelled her husband to leave and whether there is any possibility of repair. She may grasp at straws, trying to come up with a desperate deal to delay the inevitable.

A woman affected by WAS may think that her husband is just suffering from a midlife crisis that will pass, or that it's just a depression due to work problems, or that he's under the influence of a scheming girlfriend but will eventually come to his senses. With that in mind, she tries to bargain with him, or with life—"if only I could talk to him," "if only he would come to a therapist with me," "if he only knew how miserable I am, things could right themselves."

Although the husband gives no sign of any evidence to the contrary, the wife hangs on to the hope that he will realize how much she means to him. Then, she could wake up from the nightmare, "work on" the marriage and retrieve their future together. She may be banging her head against a brick wall, but it will take a lot for her to accept the message of his words and deeds—that it's over. As painful as that is, it's also liberating because it permits her to re-tool her thinking and start taking her future into her own hands.

Shawna, 38 years old and married for twelve years, experienced a dramatic shift in her feelings as soon as she learned about her husband's affair:

> About a week after he'd announced that the marriage was over, I found a cell phone I didn't know he had and looked at the text messages. I discovered that he'd been deceiving me and was with someone else. The instant I found out, it was like a switch flipped. All my love for him turned into disgust. So, it wasn't a matter of getting over him or nursing a broken heart in the classic sense. It was the psychological battle of making sense of what had happened.

The second of the **Seven Steps for Moving Forward** that must be accomplished before you can move on from the Tsunami and Thunderstorm stages is Step 3: "Integrate the fact that your husband has changed irrevocably and is beyond caring for your welfare." Women just can't understand how someone can switch horses midstream—how the man who was HUSBAND weeks earlier can become so disinterested and disengaged. The totality of that change is a mystery of the human heart and almost impossible to relate to unless you've experienced it yourself. Loving feelings do sometimes die like a fire that has gone out. You can puff on it all you want, but it won't re-ignite. Once there's nothing left in it for him, the runaway husband stops caring.

To achieve Step 3, you have to accept that even if you can't understand how it happened, your husband has had a change of heart and has nothing left to offer you. After thirty-four years of marriage, Kay was struggling to integrate that change:

The other interesting bit—he has changed. As my friend
Jean says, "Who took Gerald and who is this guy left in his
place?" Many of our friends have told me that the Gerald
they see today is not the Gerald of a couple of months ago.
My Jungian friends tell me that this is his "shadow" self
taking over his "ego." In other words, everything that he
repressed in his personality over the last thirty-four years is
flooding out, in a tsunami of nastiness toward me, and a lot
of weird behavior toward our kids, families and friends.

Perhaps the explanation of Dr. Paul McKenna and Dr. Hugh
Willbourn, in *How to Mend a Broken Heart*, will help in the process of accepting that all the Geralds have changed irrevocably.
They wrote that it is the *future* relationship that is important in a
person's life, not the past one.

People who don't experience heartbreak at the end of a
relationship have already left emotionally. Often they
already have someone else to go to, a "better" future already
planned. They have thought about it over and over again
and reinforced the neural pathways so that their new, exciting future feels very real. The old relationship is coded very
differently in their minds. They see it as a piece of history
to which they are no longer attached. This explains why the
length of a relationship is not always equal to the amount
of upset at the end. It's the future planning you do, whether
conscious or unconscious, that determines your attachment
to a person.

You still have the videotape in your head of your former husband playing a central role in your future, while he has recast his
version, replacing you with someone else. It's time now for you to
remove those images from your data bank and here's a little
exercise to help you do it. Think about how your husband looked
as you remember him and label the feelings that come up. They

may be very mixed at this point and include anger, hurt, sadness, longing and just a sick feeling. Now tell yourself that you're reacting to the physical memory of the old Gerald as you *knew* him (past tense), but the current Gerald is already a different man. One woman wrote, "It was like my husband was abducted by aliens and replaced by a total, incomprehensible stranger." What feelings arise when you think about strangers, for example, some unknown guy you may have passed on the street? I'll bet that those feelings are pretty neutral. Your husband has become a stranger and the man who looks like him is someone to whom you no longer have access. "Gerald" has left the premises!

The Affair Partner

While I was married, I had a running joke that I'd repeat whenever I went away on a trip without my husband. I'd quip that I didn't have to worry that he'd be lonely while I was away because he'd be having fun with "Dolores"—his make-believe girlfriend. To me, that was a riot—that *my* husband could ever possibly have a girlfriend was so far-fetched, I thought it was a really funny joke. A few months before he left, he asked me to stop making that joke—it offended him. Little did I know that there'd really been a "Dolores" for years and she'd been sleeping in my bed!

I'm going to devote a small amount of ink here to the bit player in this drama, the affair partner. Although she may loom large in your fantasy life or even in your actual life if you have children going back and forth, she's actually just a prop in this play. And she's not what you'd expect. Another one of the surprising things I learned from SWAP participants is how consistent the type of actress is for this role.

The night my husband told me he was moving in with his girlfriend, I knew exactly the kind of woman she'd be. I assumed that she was another university professor, someone sophisticated and accomplished. I pictured them living the high life together in her beautiful home in the posh French side of town. But I quickly learned from friends who'd met her that I was wrong. In actuality, she was a mousy-looking woman, fourteen years his junior, a former student who lived in a small apartment in a part of town that my husband actively scorned.

The consensus among SWAP participants seems to be that the affair partner is almost always significantly younger (one was *forty-one years younger* than one of the wives), almost always lower in social status (if he's the business owner then she's the receptionist, if he's the parson then she's a member of the congregation, if he's a professor then she's a student, if he's a doctor then she's a patient, a bartender, the babysitter, the cleaning lady) and certainly no trophy wife. I know this sounds like sour grapes, but it is remarkable how many women were baffled by their husband's choice of such an ordinary gal. Here's a bunch of the many descriptions about how uninspiring that "other woman" was:

- "What surprised me the most is that she is uneducated and not very bright."
- "The affair partner was fat and very dull and plain. I could not understand why he left me for her."
- "She is the last person I (and everyone else) would have expected him to be attracted to."
- "She's as dumb as a stump, not at all attractive, and has nothing to offer, and therefore the last person I would think EX would be interested in."
- "She was about as homely as the night is long. It's hard to know what to do with the fact that my husband left me for an ugly woman!"
- "Without wanting to sound arrogant, she is less attractive, less professionally successful and her personality is less effervescent."
- "She's a crazy lady, similar to his mother. She's alcoholic, pretty nutty, twelve years younger, not educated. I don't know what he's doing with her."

- "She's physically very unattractive—190 lbs—pear-shaped. She's downright ugly!"

One theory put forth by some SWAP participants was that their husbands left because they needed an ego boost from an adoring woman who could in no way be a threat to them. The choice of a junior achiever is also consistent with the speculation that some runaway husbands feel threatened by their wife's accomplishments.

There's a double deception involved when the affair partner was also a friend of the abandoned wife, and this occurred in several cases. Melanie, married thirty years, was shocked to learn that her close friend was the faceless stranger who'd exploded apart her marriage.

The affair was devastating because she had been a friend for so long and just days before the discovery, I had helped her with some sewing and she'd hugged me for helping her! The affair had been going on physically for over a year, but the attraction and dallying had been there for years. He had been coming home from work hours late and climbing into bed with me after seeing her. It was just so smarmy and far too close. Had she been a stranger, I would have seen it as a painful indiscretion, but this was unforgivable.

Looking at the affair partner's role, some idealistic SWAP participants were of the opinion that women should have more solidarity with other women and not get involved with married men. As to the outcome of those affairs, it seems as though their durability was random. Some of the runaway husbands married their affair partners and remain together years later, and some of those relationships fractured.

Is It Really Over?

If you're having trouble accepting that it's really over, ask yourself these questions:

- Have I seen any evidence of warmth, tenderness, caring or regret on the part of my former spouse since he left?

If the answer is no, let it go. If the answer is yes, ask yourself this:

- Has the tenderness I've received been consistent and long lasting over weeks or months?

If the answer is no, let it go. If the answer is yes, ask yourself this:

- Do I truly believe that the positive attention he's showing me is due to his sincere love for me or is it more likely an insurance policy to keep his options open in case things fizzle with his girlfriend?

If the answer to the first part of that question is no, let it go.

CHAPTER 10

The Big Fridge

Journal entry: Had a bad night. Fell asleep right away but woke up in the middle of the night obsessing. I was repeating the words "twenty-one years" and "six years" over and over in my mind. Trying to be Zen. When I got up today, I decided to go for a walk on the mountain. A bit concerned that I would run into *them* but, what the hell. It was a transcendent experience. It was a lovely morning—the air, the light, the sun, everything was there to comfort me. I realized that although I lost my husband, no one could take *this* away from me. I decided to say hello to everyone I passed and did. I felt joy and sadness. I enjoyed my walk and came home feeling better.

The Ice Storm Stage, typically the longest to resolve, is a period when time slows down and the world feels hard, cold, unrecognizable and unforgiving. You feel frozen and, because recovery looks a long way off, you wonder if you'll ever feel normal again. You're experiencing battle fatigue and may find that your mind keeps whirring with obsessive thoughts like an old-fashioned computer that refuses to shut down. The intensity of this stage eventually starts to lighten as you enter the Fog Stage, in which, although still very much in the thick of it, you can see patches of sunlight peeking through. That's because your mind is slowly coming around to accept that this hell won't last forever.

In this chapter, you'll gain access to the *Big Fridge*. I know that food may be the last thing on your mind right now, but the *Big Fridge* nurtures you in a different way. It's stocked with treats—coping tricks and recovery strategies—to help you keep moving in a positive direction toward your new life. You may not be in the mood for every morsel inside, but, like a real fridge, you can pick and choose what appeals to you at the moment. I would only offer you things that are nutritious to your soul, so everything on every shelf is good for you!

Obsession

Twenty-one years—six years—twenty-one years—six years. Twenty-one is the number of years that I was married. Six is the number of years of my husband's affair. I could just as easily been fixated on the number three. It was three days prior to my book launch that he left. Or my mind might have latched on to the title of the book his girlfriend wrote and dedicated to him—*Dirty Sex*. Or on the long dark hair that I found in the bathtub the day I returned from the book tour. These are the elements of deception that define my story. In the early months, try as I might, I couldn't stop my thoughts from constantly flitting around them like a psychotic hummingbird, trying to extract meaning from those supercharged words. Without a doubt, the most disturbing feature of a woman's state of mind in the early stages of WAS and throughout the Ice Storm Stage is the prevalence of intrusive thoughts and relentless obsessing.

The fact that your mind is stuck in overdrive is a direct result of you having experienced a trauma. In trauma, the mind's normal thinking process is flooded and temporarily damaged. To insure our survival, humans have a primitive need for our lives to have a reliable form and consistent meaning. Without it, we cannot prepare adequately for the future. In extreme cases, being completely unprepared for what's to come could lead to death.

—

For example, imagine that you have slipped into a twilight zone and life has become totally unpredictable. Today, it's sunny and 80 degrees; tomorrow, it will be snowing and the temperature will be zero. You're heading out this morning on a canoe trip wearing shorts and a tee shirt, planning to spend the night in a tent. However, in this unpredictable universe, the temperature will start to drop during the night so that by tomorrow morning, your life will be in danger due to exposure. Without the knowledge necessary to plan for your tomorrows, you are unable to protect yourself from harm. The ability to predict the broad strokes of your future based on an understanding of your life at the present moment is a fundamental requirement for feeling safe.

You probably had some basic understanding of events and motivations of people close to you until the moment of your husband's unexpected revelation. Your mind suffered a shock due to the incomprehensible nature of that information. I can't stress enough how essential it is for our lives to have meaning. We've already talked about the structural changes to the brain as a result of overwhelming stress. The obsessing and intrusive thoughts that result are the brain's clumsy attempt to make sense of the world in order to keep you safe. Your loyal brain thinks that if it re-examines the data about what happened hundreds of times, maybe it can accomplish its job of making meaning of these recent events and give you some protection. So it keeps scanning the files over and over, day and night, until you're begging for it to stop. Like the magic broom in *The Sorcerer's Apprentice*, once the spell has been cast, it's destined to carry out its task whether you like it or not. As 51-year-old Genevieve wrote: "The hardest part, initially, was not being able to stop thinking, every minute, every second, about what had happened. Waking up, day after day, and suddenly realizing that no, it wasn't just a bad dream, he had really left; that the bottom had fallen out of my life."

So, that's the process, now what's the content? What are we all thinking about in the middle of the night? Here are some examples of the things women obsess about:

- *Instant replay*—you relive the pressure-point events, such as the moment of the revelation or the misery of sending your child to spend the weekend at Daddy's girlfriend's house for the first time.
- *Sherlock Holmes*—you parse through everything your husband said or did trying to find a shred of meaning.
- *If onlys*—you rethink your actions as a wife prior to the end, or things you said or did after it was over, which fills you with regret and a burning wish to roll back time and do things differently.
- *Fantasy retribution*—you imagine the devastating things you could say or do that will be sure to bring your ex to his knees, if only you had the chance ... which you don't and never will.
- *Awfulizing*—you keep imaging that other horrible things will happen to you that will hurt and humiliate you and seal your miserable fate so you will never enjoy another happy day in your life.

Those are cheery thoughts to keep you company during your day, aren't they? No wonder we all get to the point where we are holding our heads and shouting, "STOP!" We feel we're at the mercy of these harpies, buzzing around us, ready to attack the second we are not completely distracted. You're most vulnerable when you are not involved in some activity that demands your attention. For me, vacuuming was hell—a guaranteed playground for my thoughts to run amok.

Fortunately, I developed a number of coping tricks and recovery strategies that you can use to tame those harpies, at least some of the time. Now we're ready to open the **Big Fridge,** so you can grab a new way of thinking or behaving that will give you some relief. These are field tested by me and found to be helpful for regaining equilibrium in the short run until time can do its magic and take you to a better mental place. And you can scramble them up. No one item will satisfy all of the time, but the variety inside will give you plenty of options from which to choose.

The Big Fridge, Part 1:
Quick 'n Dirty Coping Tricks and Recovery Strategies

First I'm going to offer you some *quick 'n dirty* techniques that will help to speedily quiet those unruly thoughts. Then we'll talk about the *life-affirming coping tricks* that will help you make in-depth changes in your outlook which will relieve the pressure in a more fundamental way. The aim of the first set of techniques is to clear your mind a little and move your thinking away from areas of pain toward a state of neutrality. They will give you more control so you can protect yourself from the intensity of the obsessive thoughts, and develop a cushion of distance from them.

I will be asking you to use your imagination, a powerful resource in your arsenal of tools for recovery, to implement both sets of techniques. As simple as they may appear, if you embrace them and try to put them into practice, you'll find that they work. Remember that it may be hard at first to turn your thoughts away from those strong negative magnets that attract them, and, like anything of value, it will take practice to incorporate these skills into your toolbox. If one really speaks to you and you use it often, it will gain in strength, helping you to reclaim more of your mind's territory from the clutches of obsessive thinking. Or, at the very least, you may get a chuckle as you see yourself trying!

Sweep, Sweep, Sweep!
Imagine that your mind is a small, wooden-floored room that keeps getting all dusty and dirty with your negative thoughts. Now visualize a tiny, inch-tall cleaning lady with an old-fashioned twig broom, whose job it is to keep the place spic 'n span. As your thoughts keep drifting back into dangerous territory, wake up the tiny cleaning lady snoozing in your brain and ask her to "sweep, sweep, sweep" away those pesky thoughts! Imagine her working away furiously, tidying up the floor and sweeping all that unwanted muck out the door.

Put a Name to It
This simple but effective suggestion helps you separate yourself
from intrusive thoughts. When you realize that your mind is on
autopilot, drifting off course where you don't want it to go, say
to yourself, "I'm obsessing!" By labeling what you're doing, you
position yourself as a spectator, observing what's going on inside
your head, rather than being helplessly immersed in it.

Barking Dog
Similar to *Put a Name to It,* this one provides you with some
distance from those demanding voices. Think of the cacophony of
thoughts in your head as a scary dog barking at you while it's
chained up to a fence next to the sidewalk. As you continue down
the street past his racket, just glance at him but know that he can't
hurt you—it's just noise—and then keep on walking.

Shake It Off
While we're on the topic of canines, here's another very simple
option for breaking out of a bad mind-set. You know how a wet
dog shakes from head to tail in that goofy way to dry himself off?
Well, when you need to lift yourself out of a funk, stand up and
literally shake it off. "Shake, shake, shake" from head to toe,
good and hard. Waggle your arms, bobble your head, jiggle your
derrière (but remember to remove your glasses first!) It's guaranteed to break the spell at least a little bit. Try it now!

Paint the Wall
This technique enables you to manage those rotten bad feelings
you walk around with. Picture yourself vigorously painting all
those angry, hurt, pent-up feelings in strong colors on a great
big wall. Use your whole body, jabbing and stroking until the wall
is violent with color. Stand back and take a good look at the turmoil exteriorized. Then imagine grabbing a roller, dipping it in a
tray of thick white paint and rolling it criss-cross and up and
down until the wall is covered all over with a field of pure white.

Stand back again and let yourself exhale. Then inhale and breathe in the clean paint smell!

Pour Some Steel in It
Try this visualization any time you need an extra boost of courage. Imagine pouring some steel down your spine. That will help you straighten up, toughen up and not be too much of a wimp!

Two Ways to Deal with Anger
Adopt the motto, "Living well is the best revenge."

Harness the Wind! Use your anger to become a fighter for your life—turn the "hurt" anger into "empowered" anger. If there's a storm raging, you'll want to have a windmill to create power.

Three Special Techniques for Getting Back in Control of Your Life

Advance Your Cause
First, define what your "cause" is in life—what is your immediate goal? Is it something concrete, like emptying the house of your ex-husband's belongings, or something more long term and abstract, like getting a better job? Make sure that it's a definable action so that you'll know when you've accomplished it (e.g., you'll know when his things are no longer in the closet, or you'll know when you've re-worked your resume). Then, do something every day that will advance your cause. At night when you get into bed, do a tally of how far along you have come toward advancing your cause.

Wait a Day
When you're upset, you may want to react quickly, but as tempting as it is, don't act on impulse. Think through the long-term

implications of your actions and ask yourself whether this is the smart thing to be doing right now. Develop self-control and act with your head as well as your heart. In other words, *don't press "send" while you're still in your pyjamas!*

Make a Mantra
Choose three words that describe the optimum state of mind you'd like to be in and repeat them to yourself whenever you feel stressed, lost or confused. They will act as shorthand to remind you of how you should be thinking and will replace other, more destructive thoughts. For example, if you know you will be seeing your former husband at your daughter's graduation from elementary school, you might make a mantra for yourself like "Calm, focused, confident." As you make your way to the school, repeat your mantra to yourself. You'll be pleasantly surprised at how it will prepare you for the upcoming encounter. It's impossible to think of two things at the same time, so your mantra will replace more disturbing thoughts like "Oh my God, I really hate seeing him."

Stacey, in her mid-fifties and married twenty-seven years when her husband left, found using a mantra really helped her accept her new life alone:

> I wrote LET IT GO on index cards and placed them everywhere I was likely to look. I put one on my bathroom mirror. I put one on my nightstand. I put one on the fridge door. I taped one to the dashboard of my car. I put one on my desk at school. I tucked one inside my lesson plan book. I put one in my purse. I whispered it to myself even as I lie in the dark, crying myself to sleep night after night. I said it over and over in my mind while walking through the mall or shopping for groceries. That constant re-affirmation of doing the only thing I really could do was a great help to me. I guess it helped me begin to think along the lines that he was not in total control of my life, that I had some free will too—that I could do something for myself. I could LET IT GO.

The Big Fridge, Part 2: Life-Affirming Coping Tricks and Recovery Strategies

The purpose of the following techniques and strategies is to stimulate a deeper level of change. They require that you adopt a more holistic view of your life, one that takes into account your long-term future and is not only focused on the here and now. It will be easier for you to put the trauma of WAS into perspective if you come to believe that, no matter how old you are at the moment, there's still plenty of living to do, so you might as well find some way to enjoy it.

My therapist suggested the following technique to me and now I use it with my own clients. It has a Zen flavor to it because it is about accepting your life with an attitude of interest but without too much attachment. It's similar to some of the others already mentioned because it's also about creating a distance between yourself and the pain you are experiencing.

Scenes from a Train

Think of the events of your life as scenery that you're observing from the window of a train. As you sit there watching it all pass by, note that the landscape out your window is constantly changing. There is always something new waiting for you on this journey.

When you're having a dark day, it helps to think of your life in this way. Sometimes you'll be totally immersed in the intensity of the moment, making it hard to believe that you'll ever feel better. But the approach to life that defines a mature person is the ability to have a long view—to know that whatever you are experiencing in the moment, whether good or bad, is transient, and the future always comes. The mistaken belief that your present reality will define your whole life leads to a lot of suffering. As crummy as you may be feeling, it helps to know that it will pass.

I have long used the following variation of *Scenes from a Train* to help clients who are struggling, and this one might also help you:

Life as a River
I suggest you think of your life as a long river you are traveling down on a sturdy raft. Sit back and observe the activity taking place on the banks as your journey continues. You can't really control the flow of the water so don't try—just accept the things that happen. Don't be afraid of what life brings you but instead keep keenly aware and interested in your story as it unfolds.

Your Thoughts as a Playground
Author Joe Barry McDonagh, panic disorder coach, wrote about how the effort to suppress intrusive thoughts actually has the opposite effect—it causes those thoughts to reoccur. "This reoccurrence of the thought has been termed the 'rebound effect.' Simply put: the more you try suppressing a thought, the more the unwanted thought keeps popping up (rebounding). Next time the fearful thought comes to mind, do not push it away. This is important. Tell yourself that that is fine and that the thought can continue to play in your mind if it wishes, but you are not going to give it much notice and you are certainly not going to qualify it by reacting with fear."

The key here is to notice the disturbing thought without associating it with a fear response. For example, if you saw a flock of pigeons in a town square, you might vaguely register—"oh, pigeons"—somewhere in your brain without any feelings at all. But for someone phobic about pigeons, that encounter might be the most terrifying thing imaginable. The fearful person becomes hyperaware of the movement of the birds and experiences a paralyzing emotional response. It's not that the birds are inherently scary—it's the meaning that is given to them that makes them a threat.

The same is true of your reaction to your ex-husband. He's just an ordinary guy to most people, but it's his potential to hurt you that makes him threatening. When thoughts and intense feelings about your ex surface, don't try to control them. By permitting your mind to become a playground for those thoughts, little by little the emotional punch they pack will begin to diminish.

You will learn to separate the thoughts (the pigeons) from the reaction (the fear).

Charlotte Joko Beck, author of *Everyday Zen*, expands on this concept in her discussion of the process by which painful thoughts naturally resolve themselves:

> I don't think that we ever let go of anything. I think what we do is just wear things out ... The best way to let go is to notice the thoughts as they come up and to acknowledge them. "Oh, yes, I'm doing that one again"—and without judging, return to the clear experience of the present moment. Just be patient. We might have to do it ten thousand times, but the value for our practice is the constant return of the mind into the present, over and over and over. Don't look for some wonderful place where thoughts won't occur. Since the thoughts basically are not real, at some point they get dimmer and less imperative and we will find there are periods when they tend to fade out because we see they are not real. They will just wither away in time without our quite knowing how it happened.

So there you have it—the **Big Fridge!** You can see that it's very well stocked with all sorts of tasty, nutritious items. Open it anytime and sample something new. Some things may be appealing today; others will tempt you tomorrow. There are coping tricks and recovery strategies sprinkled through the book, so you should be able to find plenty to help you move forward. But before we close the fridge door for now, here's a visualization that's sure to calm your mind.

A Safe Place
You may already be familiar with this lovely technique, which originated in the field of hypnotherapy. Give yourself at least five minutes when you will not be disturbed to create your special place and anchor it in your heart.

1 Start by sitting comfortably, closing your eyes and
   focus on breathing deeply.
2 Imagine a place of immense beauty, either real or
   fantasy. It may be a room or enclosed courtyard or
   some other structure, or you can envision yourself
   in a natural setting.
3 Slowly look around yourself, enjoying the light and
   color and all the visual elements.
4 Allow yourself to become aware of sensations on your
   skin—enjoy the stirring of a breeze or the warmth of
   the sun, for example.
5 Now focus your mind on the pleasing scent of this
   place—the perfume in the air of a room, the fresh
   smell of the woods, the ozone scent of the sea.
6 Awaken your ears to sounds filling the air—whatever
   you may want. You can include music, chimes, distant
   gongs, the whoosh of the waves or the splashing of
   a lively brook.
7 Now, if you want company, fill this place with people
   who bring you joy. Invite only those who make you
   feel good.
8 Bring into your safe place those precious things that
   you cherish—a book, a photograph, a piece of jewelry—whatever is guaranteed to make you smile. And
   don't forget your dog or cat!
9 Wherever you have imagined yourself—lying on a
   comfy sofa, strolling in the sun on a beach, sitting on a
   rock at the top of a mountain trail—know that YOU
   ARE SAFE! Relax and just enjoy being here—this
   place exists inside of you. Nothing bad can happen to
   you here.
10 Return often. The more often you visit your safe place,
   the easier it will be to get in touch with all the richness
   it brings to you. Whenever you are suffering, close
   your eyes, turn your focus inward, and it's but a short
   journey to your safe place.

CHAPTER II

Your Personal Narrative

Twenty-one years—six years—these words also served as the framework that I fitted my story around as I told it and retold it to concerned relatives, friends, neighbors and acquaintances. Each chosen word had a hidden meaning—twenty-one years (we were married a long time)—six years (that rat's affair started even before his transplant!)—three days (after an affair of six years and all I did for him, couldn't he have waited three days till after my book launch?). The title of the book his girlfriend wrote, *Dirty Sex*, the long dark hair, etc.—they all supported my narrative about how shabby his behavior was, how narcissistic he is and how poorly he treated me. There was a cold comfort in repeating those words in my mind, and I found myself needing to say them when I told my story to uninitiated others.

Eventually, however, I realized that reiterating that story (and I know that every woman in the study has her own version of such a narrative) was ultimately an act of desperation. I needed to continually reaffirm to myself the callousness of his behavior in order to justify the magnitude of my hurt. I was punctuating it to myself but also to the world at large; it would do me good if the facts of my narrative stimulated a chorus of outrage. After a long while and with great effort, I trained myself not to need to elicit a shocked response from acquaintances who inquired about my husband's health, and to simply say, "Oh, we're no longer together."

What's the first thing you do when your car has been rammed from behind while you're stopped at a light? You look for a witness! We all want a witness to confirm our reality—"It wasn't my fault! I was standing still! He'll tell you—he saw it all!" We need someone who can act as an impartial observer, not only to describe the event to the police, but also to confirm our own perception of what happened. In WAS, when our reality is under siege by the person we trusted the most, the word of the witness is invaluable. So we turn to our friends to supply an outsider testament that verifies our perceived reality.

We all live our lives in a fishbowl, under the scrutiny of others whose opinions contribute significantly to our self-definition. A positive assessment from the community of friends is far more crucial to women than it is to men. Growing up, girls are commended for accommodating others, whereas boys are often praised for independent achievement. In my work as a psychotherapist, I find that the majority of women who come into my office are struggling to feel good about themselves and are very vulnerable to criticism. Weren't we all trained to be good little girls, trying to get the pat on the head from someone who had the power to say if we were good or bad? An unanticipated marital breakdown is such a public event that the judgment of friends, colleagues and family is very important.

Priceless

The first thing I did on the "I bought fish" night was to get in my car and somehow drive across town to the home of our friends, Andrea and Jim. I sat in their living room for twenty minutes, an untouched glass of white wine warming in my hand. I assume I told them what happened, but really have no recollection of what I said. Then I drove home. The next day, Andrea told me what she and Jim did after I left. They took the six-pack of non-alcoholic beer that they always had on hand for my teetotaller husband and ceremoniously poured the contents of each bottle, one by one, down the kitchen sink. Hearing about that symbolic act of solidarity warmed my heart and cheered me up, and even now, it still brings a smile to my lips.

Not long ago, I gave a workshop about Wife Abandonment Syndrome in Toronto. Madeleine, one of the women attending, had been left by her husband twenty-three years earlier. Although remarried long ago, she attended my workshop in the hope of finally solving the mystery of why her first husband fled the marriage in the incomprehensible way he did. Her best friend, Ava, had come to the talk with her, and when we got on the topic of friends, Madeleine shared her story:

> Every night for about a year after my husband left, I went over to my neighbors, Ava and Alex, after dinner and sat in their kitchen and cried. They both worked and had small children, and I don't know how they did it! One night, I decided I couldn't interrupt their lives any more and decided to stay at home. The next night, Alex rang my doorbell to ask why I hadn't come the night before and to tell me that they were concerned about me. He asked me to please come over to their place. Talk about feeling loved!

There were many stories from SWAP participants about human life rafts like Ava and Alex who made sacrifices and did selfless things, like flying across the country at a moment's notice to be with a grieving friend. These "angels" arrived, tissues and casseroles in hand, to pack up the house for a hurry-up move, walk the dog, paint the new apartment, push food in front of the recalcitrant eater and spend hours playing Lego on the floor with the bewildered kids. Most of the women in the study received spectacular support, as did I, from a circle of friends who were scandalized by the behavior of the runaway husband. Their stories can be summed up by this contribution from Melanie, married thirty years:

Friends have saved my sanity! They have kept me busy, kept me social and "out." They have listened to the rants and the "whys" and the "what could I have done differentlys." More than anything I can see how much a woman's female friends count! Women seem to know how to share pain, empathize, make you laugh at the situation and yourself and just to BE there! It took about six months of TLC from my children and these wonderful women to haul me out of the abyss. Oh, I worked hard, too ... but they are the rungs on that ladder! They are the reason I'm as healthy as I am right now.

As I stated earlier, one of the primary roles of friends and family at this point is to validate the reality of the abandoned wife. Since your mind is not functioning well, you look to the reactions of others around you to confirm for you the magnitude of what has happened. But more important, you need to hear from them that it wasn't your fault and you *are* a good person. For example, on hearing my news, a friend said that she believes that there is right and wrong in this world, and leaving the way my husband did was just plain wrong. I liked that. She said it with emphasis—it was clear. Even my muddled mind could understand that. Other stuff that I liked to hear was the immediate reaction of a male friend who said, "How could anyone leave *you?*," and another whose first response was, "I'm going to come over there and beat him up for you!" Yay! That felt good. A SWAP participant wrote, "One of the best things my friends all did was to concur with my bewilderment—nobody had ANY idea that this was coming, nobody had seen a SINGLE sign or clue. That made me feel a lot better."

What I didn't want to hear was the position of a friend who said that he wanted to remain neutral. No. "Neutral" didn't feel right. I understand why friends try to stay out of the fray, but honestly, "neutral" didn't impress me.

Inconsolable

Not every friend, of course, has the courage or skill to comfort you with the exactly right words; there are no ritualized phrases for them to murmur as there would be at a funeral. The rawness of your suffering will make some people feel profoundly helpless or even completely blow them away. A friend who has experienced a similar rejection risks joining in your downward spiral if she gets too involved, but may not know how to tell you that she needs to make herself scarce without appearing uncaring. Six months after my husband left, I invited a close friend out to a French restaurant for her birthday, looking forward to having a chance to talk. I was flummoxed when she showed up with her cousin. It took me about a year to realize that although the end of *her* marriage had taken place long before, she was still not up to hearing about mine. She'd enlisted her cousin's help to make sure the conversation stayed light.

Along the same lines, Siobhan, a SWAP participant from Ireland, wrote, "I lost my best friend through this. She was pregnant through the tail end of it and I don't blame her for not wanting to be around an anxiety driven, depressed and emotionally devastated woman. She had already had two miscarriages. We drifted apart. I miss her but I don't hold any malice towards her as we both had to follow our own paths."

You may want to be left alone, but it's not usually the healthiest course to take. Although some confident friends will ignore your request for solitude and insist that you come out with them, others will think that respecting your wishes is the way to go. This dilemma is eloquently described in an email that I received from Josie, the dear friend of a WAS sufferer who was in the midst of the worst of it. Josie and two other friends were trying their best to help (and doing a phenomenal job), but it was taking a toll. Josie wrote about what it was like to try to support her friend:

> At first she was so devastated and shattered that all she could do was cry. She was confused and kept looking to us

for answers we just couldn't provide—all we could do was
listen and sympathize. We were a bit in shock ourselves since
we all knew her husband well and couldn't believe he would
do such a thing to her. It was awful to watch her in such
pain—both physical and emotional. Helpless is probably
the best way to describe our feelings at that time.

Every day at least one of us called or emailed to check-up
on her and to let her know that we were here for her. We
didn't know what else to do. Overall I think we tried to follow her lead—be there when she needed to talk and leave
her alone when she needed some time to think. We tried to
support her decisions without being judgmental and tried
not to stress her out more by forcing her to go through the
emotional stages of this whole thing faster than she was
ready to—although I have to say that was a bit difficult
and frustrating for us at times.

Over the past few weeks we have made sure that she has
seen her doctor (she hasn't been eating or sleeping), gotten
together several times to hang out and chat, encouraged
her to go to the gym and invited her out for walks, coffee,
movies, dinner, etc., and offered to go with her to see her
lawyer and accountant to advocate for her—stuff like that.
Tried to keep her busy and feeling supported.

Now since you asked what it's been like to go through
this as a friend, I have to be honest with you. I feel absolutely horrible for admitting this, but on occasion, I've resented
the time all this has been taking away from the precious little
I have with my own family. I've spent an awful lot of time
on the phone lately listening to my friend or talking to the
other two women about what we can do to help or what has
gone on that day. I truly do want to help her and be there
for her—she is a good friend and I take friendships very seriously—but not at the expense of my family. I have promised
to be there when she needs me, but on occasion that has
meant rearranging or dropping plans that I've made at

home. My husband is great—he's very understanding, but I do feel a bit conflicted at times.

I'm sure many of my friends would echo Josie's sentiments; I was pretty wretched for a very long time. They'd recognize that helpless feeling, the aching desire to make it better and Josie's contrite admission that sometimes it was all too much and she resented it. That's what psychologists call "compassion fatigue"—the loss of sympathy for the suffering of others experienced by caregivers as a result of the demands made on them. It's normal for your friends to get to the point of feeling swamped because the crisis period is so protracted. Just when things start to settle down, there's sure to be a new calamity that whips you back into a state of high anxiety so you have to start making those frantic late-night S.O.S. calls again.

If you're lucky enough to be close with your family, compassion fatigue may not play as much of a role because they (and your *very* closest friends) would go to the ends of the earth to soothe your pain. Here are some thoughts from women whose relatives were always ready to comfort them when they were inconsolable:

- "I'm very close with my family. I remember when I was still thinking maybe counseling could save my marriage, though it was obvious it wouldn't, my father saying 'Naomi, he doesn't want to be with you anymore.' It was like a slap up-side the head, but it worked. My mom came to Asheville and made me soup and ginger ale while I lay on the floor and cried. She was her usual strong, but non-judgmental self."
- "My sister spent hours & hours & hours & more hours consoling me on the phone from 1,000 miles away."
- "Whenever I began to sink into deep darkness, my mother would come over to get me out of bed to take a shower. Sometimes, she would simply lie beside me in my bed and listen. She cooked for me and did things around the house when I couldn't manage to get out of bed."

- "My older brother helped me refinance my house so that we would not have to move. The first thing my younger brother said to me was, 'You didn't deserve this!' (as opposed to calling my former husband horrible names—he did that later)."
- "My family told me they wanted to hire an assassin—stupid, but it helped!"

As much as you might want to avoid needing so much support, it's part of the recovery process—make a pledge to yourself that one day, you'll pay it forward. But for now, you can remedy the situation somewhat. First, try to spread your need for support among as many friends and family members as possible. Second, seek professional help from a counselor who understands abandonment. Third, try hard to be considerate of your friends and limit the desperate cries for help to those times when you really need it. And fourth, if you can ever think of something positive or even funny to say, be sure to tell a friend! I remember that I was determined not to be too much of a drag when I was invited out to dinners early on, so I prepared in advance by reading the newspaper and thinking up topics to talk about other than my own unrelenting misery.

There's a certain amount of ambivalence that comes into play during the Ice Storm/Fog stages. Some days you may not feel so bad, but you know it's temporary. You don't want to appear too chipper for fear that your friends will say, "Whew, that's over," and then become impatient the next time you hit the skids. Instead, you'll look pitiful in order to keep getting the consolation you need—otherwise, people will assume you're okay. There's a subtle shift during this stage of recovery in which, even though you're no longer in the depths of hell, you know you're far from well yet. What has happened is so huge that you're not ready to start moving past it. You still need the world to acknowledge your suffering.

It's a paradox—you mustn't look too strong or else you won't get the support you need. But by hanging on to that fragility, you remain weak and don't recover as quickly. Zara, twenty-five years into her second marriage when it ended, wrote, "Initially I did not want to cope. I have been strong all my life and people responded by reassuring me of my strength. Somehow, I wanted them to know just how BIG this was for me and how devastating, and the only way that seemed possible was by not coping, by being a basket case. By coping, well it felt like I was saying, 'This isn't much. It isn't that bad. I'll just get on with my life.'"

What Not to Say and What to Say Instead

As wonderful as most women reported their friends to be, there were also many stories of friends who didn't come through. Some challenged the abandoned wife's statement that she didn't see it coming. Believing that men don't really leave out-of-the-blue may have helped the friend feel more secure in her own marriage. But most friends who didn't come through missed the mark because it's very hard to understand the impact of this level of betrayal. Even many therapists don't get it!

Carol, whom I interviewed in a café in Burlington, Vermont, cited some tactless comments that stung:

> I had told an acquaintance what happened and her answer to me was "I'd kill my husband if he did that!" Another time, a friend came to visit me and her little girl asked, "Mommy, how come we don't have a house alarm like Carol?" and my friend said, "Because we have Daddy to protect us!" I still remember that! Or a neighbor, a stay-at-home mom, whose husband was gone for two days, said, "I know how you feel! I'm a single mom till Wednesday!" Puh-lease—you have no idea! So those were the times when I wanted to be bitter, and my retort would have left them lying on the ground, but I recognize that they're just clueless.

Marcy, 39 years old and married for ten years, knew that her friends and family cared but felt they couldn't truly relate to what she was going through:

On the whole, no one really understood, no one really got it.
I felt very, very alone. My parents in particular, married for
over 40 years, told me at one point they had champagne
waiting for the day the divorce was final. Although I know
they meant to be supportive with that, it told me they had
NO IDEA what this had done to me. Regardless of how
great it would be that it was over, or how much better off
I was without him, the divorce was still a death, a death
of the person I was and the dreams I had, and was nothing
to celebrate.

Here's a very special list (as told to me by SWAP participants)
of some the things people SHOULD NOT SAY when a friend or
family member has been dumped:

- *"Get over it and stop dwelling,"* which not only feels to the
  ex-wife like her enormous loss is being trivialized and she's
  not allowed her grief and anger, but also that she's doing
  this wrong.
- *"I always knew that he was not to be trusted "* and other
  negative things about him that only make the ex-wife think
  how stupid and blind *she'd* been.
- *"We never really liked him,"* which makes her wonder why
  they'd been friends with her and her ex-husband in the first
  place.
- *"You'll find someone else,"* as if the only way she'll move on
  and be happy again will be if she finds another man.
- *"It must have been a bad marriage all along,"* which implies
  that she was just not facing up to a supposed reality.
- *"At least there aren't any children involved,"* which is a double
  whammy for women who have been trying to get pregnant.
- *"It could be worse—at least you have your health,"* which
  sounds like the only thing worse is terminal illness.
- *"He's not coming back,"* told to the wife while she is still in
  shock and not ready to integrate that.

- *"The second marriage will be better than the first"*—how is that supposed to help?
- *"You're worth ten of him,"* which makes her feel like everyone knew she was with a loser all these years.
- *"It was bound to happen because you're older than him."* No explanation necessary!

Words That Can Help

Most people don't realize that it's often not necessary to say anything at all. Just being there with open ears is often enough. But there are some words that can help, and here's a special list of some the things a person SHOULD SAY if a friend or family member has been dumped:

- *"You may not be perfect, but you didn't do anything to cause him to leave like this"* helps relieve some of the guilt and self-blame that consumes an ex-wife.
- *"Don't try to make sense of this"* acknowledges that the husband's actions are incomprehensible.
- *"You're a good person and a good mom"* is a precious sentiment that helps counteract some of the negativity sent her way by her husband.
- *"Divorce is worse than death,"* spoken by a woman who had recently been widowed, meant a lot to the woman left.
- *"I'm really sorry that this has happened to you"* are simple words of caring that go a long way.
- *"Talk to me!"* is the best thing a friend can say—to just listen without judgment and allow her to talk, rave, scream and cry.
- *"Don't get a new man, get a snow blower,"* spoken by a neighbor, gave the wife living solo a laugh!

CHAPTER 12

Theories

A word of advice: don't go to Paris when you've been dumped. Everywhere you turn, couples are embracing. You're standing in front of some painting at the Musée d'Orsay when a man nestles up behind the woman standing next to you. He slips his arms around her waist, buries his face in her hair and kisses her. It's excruciating. That woman was me, not so long ago. I feel the urge to ask any random man to embrace me, just so I can experience it again for a moment. I have to keep reminding myself that I had that for many years and will again in the future.

Missing Your Best Friend

This is a spirally process. When you're in your right mind, you remember who you are and the fact that life holds infinite possibilities for happiness. You know that you will recover and not always feel this bad. You're determined to take the high road so you can feel proud of yourself, in spite of it all. But then you're hurled into a different edge of the spiral and slink back into the dark night of panic, loneliness and despair. Recovery is such a complex process that you can't hold it all in your head at one time. It changes form constantly. What seemed so important at one point will appear inconsequential days later. You seesaw from hating him and wanting him dead to missing him and wanting him back. You have trouble hanging on to the memory of the cruel things your husband did and of whom he has become. You just miss him.

This alternating frame of mind is typical of the **Sun Shower Transformational Stage**, during which the wife, putting some distance from the actual abandonment, continues to work on understanding the meaning of this traumatic event. She's reached Step 6 in the **Seven Steps for Moving Forward**, and is trying to turn her focus from the past to the future. This is difficult because her mind keeps reverting to the default position—the memory of her beloved husband snaps back into place when she thinks about her life.

It's hard to break a habit, even if the habit involves loving someone who's hurt you. When you're alone and struggling, it's natural to miss the person you loved, even if you sometimes hate him. And when something special happens in your life, of course you want to talk to your best friend.

The wish to be able to tell my husband about my life was a regular feature of the early months when I found it harder to compartmentalize, but later on, it only surfaced when really big things happened to me. It flooded back a year and a half after he left, when I was invited to appear on NBC's *Today Show* in New York to talk about my book about sisters. It was a very big deal for me, and the spot went perfectly. I walked off the set pumped and excited, and just wanted to be able to call *him* and tell *him*! In the old days, he would've been so proud and happy for me. It would've felt great to triumph together. But when this unique event in my life was over and it had been an amazing success, I fought back pain waves of longing and a sense of emptiness because I had no one special person to share it with.

In this chapter, we'll continue the process of making meaning out of your husband's sudden departure by addressing what SWAP participants believe about their husband's motivation.

The Devil Made Me Do It

After all that agonizing and brain-wracking that took place during the Thunderstorm and Ice Storm stages, women in the study came up with a short list of theories as to why they believe their husbands chose to end the marriage in such a dramatic and unexplained fashion. I must admit that the word "coward" came up most frequently, but the majority of other explanations given fall into five categories:

- The bitch made him do it.
- He needed an ego boost.
- He underwent a midlife crisis.
- He was intimidated by his wife's success.
- He has a character flaw.

Some wives point the finger directly at the affair partner to explain why their husband strayed in the first place. Many were convinced that the other woman pushed hard to "get" their man, and that the attentions of this spoiler were just too tempting for him to pass up. SWAP participants described the affair partner as "working on him," "luring him away with her flirting" and "railroading him." Others said that their husband was "seduced by a married woman," "offered sex on a plate," and that "the *skank* pursued him." Lots of feelings there! Genevieve, married twenty-five years, had always encouraged her husband's trips with colleagues from work. She explained her theory about how her husband got caught:

> The simple and crass answer is that I let him run off-leash one time too many. He was on vacation in India with some friends from his office and met a woman who completely fell all over him with flattery and her "womanly wiles." She was divorced, had no income and little in the way of monetary assets, and has a serious addiction to shopping and maintaining her "beauty"—in other words, desperately in need

of a meal ticket. She was also a massage therapist. On the trip, they were staying at very expensive and exotic palaces. One of my husband's colleagues offered her a job and asked my husband to "train" her. So wow, Henry Higgins, Mr. Magoo, incense, desperate former beauty queen, throw in a massage or two, and you got love!

The comfort behind this kind of explanation for the abandoned wife is that it portrays the man as a weak but initially unwilling participant—prey rather than predator. The wife then can somewhat maintain her vision of him as having been under the evil spell of a Siren, like the Argonauts in Greek mythology. This version helps explain how the man could change so suddenly. Poor dear! It was beyond his control.

On the Pedestal

Many SWAP participants theorized that their husband's attraction to the affair partner functioned as an ego boost. There's nothing like the excitement of an illicit affair to rejuvenate a man (or woman) and make him feel sexy and desirable. We all know that in a decades-long marriage, the idealization that occurred in the courtship phase is long gone. The wife knows the truth about her husband's past. The man who is now a well-respected physician was once a hypochondriac med student convinced that he was afflicted with every disease he studied. In the eyes of a new woman who is impressed by him and doesn't know his past foibles, however, he can refashion himself midlife.

Most women don't understand how men typically depend on their wife's idealized appreciation to truly feel like a man. Roslyn, 63, was helpless in the face of her husband Brian's need for the attention of his other woman: "Looking back, I can see that he always had a high need for absolutely UNCONDITIONAL 'adoration' in the forty-two years we were married and eventually, his 35-year-old ex-student provided that. It must have been very 'flattering' to him that this attractive young woman even let a 70-year-old man PAW her—he couldn't resist—and decided he had 'fallen in love.'"

Brian "got lucky" in both senses of that term. There was no way that Roslyn, with her 63-year-old body and forty-two years of history with that man, could compete. Other women wrote:

- "He needed someone to tell him he was amazing, to feel he was the strong one in the relationship, someone who worshipped him, like his mom did. I didn't. I wanted a husband, not a hero."
- "I believe my husband left because I no longer had him on a pedestal. He has an insatiable need to be adored, and he knew I could not fill that need."
- "Later I realized I had always kind of idolized him, but when I started to feel more confident and stopped, he had to find someone to replace me."
- "I think this whole rush of falling in love, having someone pay an inordinate attention to him, hearing all his stories (which we've all heard a million times) and thinking he's 'The Man' gave him the power to just walk away."

The Halo Effect

Perhaps the most frequent reason offered by SWAP participants for their husband's departure was that he was suffering a midlife crisis. A medical dictionary defines midlife crisis as "a period of personal emotional turmoil and coping challenges that some people encounter when they reach middle age, accompanied by a desire for change in their lives, brought on by fears and anxieties about growing older." Men who haven't achieved what they'd hoped by the age of fifty or fifty-five see their opportunities for success dwindling and may get demoralized. Men who *have* made their mark may feel that all the fun is over and there's not much to look forward to. They see the young guys climbing up the ladder at their heels, and the thought of being out of the game fills them with dread. Many WAS men had complained long and hard about their jobs before they left. Their wives knew they were unhappy but thought the locus of misery was at work.

In the midst of this discomfort related to aging, a man might one day glance over at his wife and suddenly be struck by how *she's* aged. Hair streaked with grey, she's reached menopause and put on some pounds, and it reflects negatively on him. Deep in his subconscious, he may feel that if only he could throw the old fish overboard and find a new minnow, he could trick himself into believing that he's still the sexy, potent shark of his fantasy. It's a tired old cliché, but many men at this point *do* go out and buy some hot new clothes, start dying their hair and join the gym. Shortly before he left, my own sedentary husband, typically attired in worn-out, baggy jeans, proudly showed me the red top-of-the-line exercise clothes he'd bought. It seemed out of character, but not enough of a red flag to alert me to the hidden meaning of such a purchase and the fact that he would never have bought clothes like that on his own.

Priscilla, married twenty-five years, summed up the changes in her 59-year-old husband:

> He had so much going on that I think his relationship with me became part of the halo effect, i.e., "All things are bad in my life right now and I'm not having much fun. Plus I only have so many years to live and I want to be happy." Personally, I know why my husband left probably more explicitly than he does. It was about his inadequacies and not mine. You ask what they are running from. In my case, the answer is simple. He was running from himself. But he would not be able to tell you that.

Lindsay, after twenty-two years of marriage, has analyzed her husband's motivation as follows:

I think he panicked when he turned 50 (he left within two
months of his birthday). I think he was looking back and
seeing failure (though we had put together a comfortable
lifestyle) and looking ahead and realizing time was running
out. He'd had fantasies of making millions (I'm serious) and
retiring early, though he took a bankruptcy ten years ago
and has not made much of a living ever since. In leaving the
country, trying different jobs, and taking up with a much
younger woman, I think he's having a "do over" life.

The Wife's Success

A midlife crisis in a man, which leads to him feeling dissatisfied
and unhappy overall, has an important physiological component.
Jed Diamond, author of *The Irritable Male Syndrome*, clarified
the biological basis for it:

> Male menopause, also known by the more scientifically
> accepted term andropause, occurs in all men, generally
> between the ages of 40 and 55. In some men, it can occur as
> early as 35 or as late as 65. Some clinicians and researchers
> define andropause simply in terms of a decline in the male
> hormone testosterone. In my experience, andropause is like
> adolescence: All males go through it, though some have
> more symptoms than others. It is hormonally driven, but it
> is more complex than simply a shift in hormone levels. Phys-
> ical, psychological, social, and sexual changes also occur ...
> We long for love, acceptance, and approval from our part-
> ners and peers. We struggle for self-respect. We act impul-
> sively, moved by emotions we cannot name or do not
> understand.

So while women are coping with menopause, men are losing
hormones of their own. It used to be a common belief that men
are at the height of their sexual prowess at age 18 while women

peak at 40. Another cruel mismatch of life-cycle timing occurs around midlife. Men in their thirties and forties were in the building phase of their careers, while their wives may have been working sporadically, treading water through maternity leaves and child rearing. When a woman reaches her fifties, however, she's often finally freed up from childcare and may also have completed her role caring for older parents. It's finally her turn to throw her energy and creativity into her work. Her husband may have been waiting for this moment to get his wife back, but, disappointing for him, she's excited about the chance to turn her focus in another direction. So often, her career is ramping up as his is winding down, and he just doesn't like how that feels.

Here's Jed Diamond again talking about how this played out in his own relationship. His wife, Carlin, started a school at this point in her life and "seemed to blossom": "I was glad Carlin was becoming increasingly successful in her work, but I began to feel slightly uneasy. The thoughts rarely broke through the surface, but just underneath I wondered whether she would surpass me in success ... My conscious mind was delighted at her success, but my less conscious self was feeling threatened and competitive."

A man whose wife does appear to be surpassing him in life may suddenly start losing interest in her success. He liked it better the old, traditional way when he was the primary breadwinner and his wife's career was an adjunct. That was undoubtedly the case with my husband. After twenty-one years in which he brought home a much heftier salary than I could, he chose to end the marriage three days before my book launch. As much as he made the right noises about being proud of my success, he balked at the hurdle. He just couldn't face it.

Deb and Tony had both held down good jobs in advertising until a few years before he left. He lost his job unexpectedly and sort of froze after that, unable to motivate himself to find something new. Meanwhile, Deb was working frantically to make sure there was a secure income in the family. Eventually, Tony resorted to taking a much lower position with another firm and was stuck doing work that he hated. Deb wrote:

It was the type of job he'd always scorned as a position for those who couldn't make it in the "real world." That's when his real unhappiness started. He hated it with a passion and spent the next few years stuck at the lowest level in the hierarchy in the firm, despite his long years of experience. My career, on the other hand, took off. I ended up running the organization for several months, traveled a lot and generally relished what I was doing. I was making significantly more money than him at this point.

He didn't talk often about his work and actually told me that he didn't want to hear me talk about mine. I figured that he was so unhappy with his job that he didn't want to hear me natter on about my days. Interestingly, the one thing he told me several times was how funny his office mates, particularly the females, found him. This was weird to me because while he does have a very good dry sense of humor, he's never, ever been a barrel of laughs and, now, in his own words, he's "the office clown."

When Tony informed Deb that he was leaving, he told her that everything that had gone wrong in his life was due to her and that her greatest fault was that she made him feel deficient. It eventually came out that one of the laughing young females at his office who found him "funny, charming and debonair" had been more than a work colleague—she had been giggling with him all the way to the bedroom.

Character Flaws

Although it may be normal for a husband to want to leave what he perceives to be an unhappy marriage, it's the lack of remorse, indifference to the ex-wife's suffering and all the lying that shows his character in a new light. And that new light does not have a rosy hue. While I was in the thick of it, it helped me to think of my husband as having a personality disorder of some sort, but I wondered how he'd hidden it for twenty-one years. Then I realized that the very fact that he was capable of appearing loving and devoted during the six years he was having an affair was actually a symptom of that disorder. He is either a master at "splitting," a narcissist or a sociopath who does not feel remorse. Whichever one, it's not good.

My own therapist proposed the "splitting" hypothesis. The concept of splitting in psychology refers to a tendency to view things and people as only all good or all bad. People who split have trouble accepting that there can be shades of gray. How it would function in the context of WAS would be for a man to have a very positive, idealized view of his wife that then flips to a very negative one when he stops seeing her as perfect.

Another dimension of splitting would be for a man to compartmentalize his feelings so that he could justify behaving in ways that are not consistent from one situation to the next. For example, when my husband was being tender and loving with me, he meant it, even if he had just crawled out of his girlfriend's bed. When he was being loving with her, he meant that too. He was able to isolate his feelings for me from his feelings for her because he'd manufactured some justification that would make that possible.

I remember once working in therapy with a man who'd had an affair with an 18-year-old live-in nanny hired to help his wife shortly after she'd delivered their second child. He described to me the internal mechanism that permitted him to leave his exhausted wife sleeping upstairs and sneak down to the babysitter's room in the basement for a romantic middle-of-the-night tryst. He said that he took the computer chip of "wife and children" out of his head and left it on the shelf when he entered the girl's room. He'd chosen to separate his identity into parts: Part A—dutiful husband and father, and Part B—daring, sexy stud.

This man was able to lie to himself in order to tolerate the subterfuge in which he was engaged—he was able to pretend to himself that he was not a married man while he was having sex with his girlfriend. Once a person masters the ability to lie so effortlessly to himself, lying to others is a breeze. Men who fit the profile for Wife Abandonment Syndrome have lied prior to leaving (almost all were having affairs), lie at the point of leaving (fabricating justifications for their departure) and continue to lie post-separation (denying the good that existed in the marriage). It's all very confusing to women who are used to believing in their husband's honesty.

A second character-flaw explanation that SWAP participants reported was that their husband was a narcissist. One woman told me that she felt very relieved when she learned about this personality disorder and recognized how well it fit her husband. She'd felt that he always expected to get his needs met but that the needs of others were not really of interest to him. He cared about her only in terms of what she could do for him. In the 1970s, psychoanalyst Heinz Kohut developed a term for the way narcissistic people treat others. He said that they relate to other people as "self-objects." That means that the narcissistic individual experiences the role of the other person primarily to complete his identity. He does not love his wife for the woman she is as a separate person, but rather for the way she makes him feel about *himself!*

Third, at the far end of the spectrum, some wives concluded that the only way their husbands could walk away in such a cavalier fashion was if they were actually sociopaths. The primary trait of people with this diagnosis is guiltlessness. It may be hard to imagine, but sociopaths are capable of committing the most hurtful acts without feeling bad about it. They don't need to rationalize it, they don't need to make excuses to themselves; they just don't feel what you or I might feel if we acted in a way that hurt others. Sonia, married thirty-six years, found this to be the only reasonable explanation for her devoted husband's apparent guilt-free conscience at his departure: "I think he's sociopathic. There's been no remorse, and he even thinks we should all be very happy for him. He wanted the kids to meet his girlfriend right away, as if they should want to. We were a close family, and he expected them to embrace this new lover and acted hurt when they refused. He's the center of his own universe—arrogant and selfish."

Because everyone assumes that others experience guilt, it's easy for the sociopath to pretend that his or her emotions are normal. And surprisingly, rather than appearing cold and heartless as you may imagine, they sometimes are very warm and the life of the party. Martha Stout's book, *The Sociopath Next Door,* contends that a certain number of sociopaths fly under the radar, undetected as we interact with them every day. Stout, who calculates that four percent of people fall into this category, illustrated why one might miss the Machiavellian intention under the everyday veneer. She describes a typical trait as "a glib and superficial charm that allows the true sociopath to seduce other people, figuratively or literally—a kind of glow or charisma that, initially, can make the sociopath seem more charming or more interesting than most of the normal people around him." Stout was intrigued by a common belief held by the sociopaths that she studied. Rather than taking responsibility for the damage they did to others, they asserted that they themselves were the victims. WAS men in my study frequently voiced that sentiment as well.

I'm not intimating that WAS men fall into diagnosable categories like narcissistic personality disorder or sociopath, but I believe that it takes a certain kind of emotional disconnect to suddenly run away from a long-term marriage without expressing concern or remorse.

But it's not only the wives that suffer. Up till now, we have not addressed the experience of the kids who are unwittingly swept up in their parents' drama, so we'll turn our attention now to the effect of Wife Abandonment Syndrome on the lives of children.

CHAPTER 13

Collateral Damage

Children's lives, too, are turned upside down by Wife Abandonment Syndrome, and the one word that came up over and over when women described their kids' reaction was "devastated." The kids' reality has been shaken in many of the same ways that their mothers' have—the man they knew as their father may now seem very different. Don't forget that if women were in the dark about there having been anything wrong, so were the children. When Daddy suddenly moves out, the kids too are completely unprepared. The shock of the sudden dissolution of the family is compounded by the existence of the affair partner and the fact that fathers often expect the kids to immediately integrate her into their lives. Children have no time to adjust to all the changes, making the emotional fallout prolonged and intense. Here are some descriptions of kids' reactions:

- "My son (15) wouldn't get out of bed, he wouldn't go to school, he wouldn't eat, and he started smoking."
- "My daughter (16) was suicidal, as her father was her hero."
- "Our son (5) is devastated to have lost his happy family."
- "Both girls (14 and 16) have gone through an ocean of tears and been extremely angry with their dad."
- "Our son (12) cried every night for weeks. Eventually, he shut his door. He was broken-hearted. He became depressed and withdrawn."

- "The children (13, 11 and 6) were very upset, very let down by their father whom they adored, and found it difficult to have to deal with the new woman/now step-mum and her boys, with whom they don't get along."

Seventeen-year-old Alexandra was heading out to a party one evening when she stopped in at her mom's room to say "bye." One look at her mom's face told her that something was very wrong. When she heard the news, Alex was shocked and upset; the fact that her father had left seemed unimaginable because her parents' relationship had seemed perfectly normal and she'd never seen them fight. In her questionnaire, she wrote, "To be 100% honest, i went to the party anyway and just got drunk to the point that i passed out so i could get away from the situation." When she came home, much as she hoped she'd imagined it, she quickly realized that her life had been transformed into a grim new reality from which she couldn't escape.

Six months later, she says that her dad seems upset. He calls and sends her a lot of emails, but she doesn't respond. Although the youngest in the family, she carries the weight of everyone's grief on her shoulders:

> i feel like i'm the only sane one in my family, that i'm the
> one holding it all together, my brother went into a really deep
> depression, my mom was a skeleton and my dad was out of
> the picture, so i just try to keep everyone happy, it wears me
> down all the time, but i can't let anyone know because i feel
> like i get so frustrated when my mom is upset in front of me
> that i don't want to do the same thing back to her.

At the age of 17, Alex is already jaded. In answer to a question about whether her views of marriage have changed as a result of what happened in her family, she wrote, "My views have changed 100%. Before all of this i was such a strong believer in true love will conquer it all and that that will make everything okay. But not any more. i've realized how much work a marriage is and should be and i don't even know if i want to get married now because i really could never handle this situation."

Alexandra was successful in camouflaging from her family the extent to which she really was struggling. Her mom, Mary Jane, wrote in her questionnaire, "Alex struggled with seeing me fall apart for the first week. She had some acting out moments, but she fortunately has a good support group and strong faith that is getting her through. She continues on with life like a high school student should, having fun."

Mary Jane describes her kids' attitude toward their dad and his response to it:

> Needless to say my religious daughter sees no gray ... "You took vows so you try everything to work on those vows and adultery is a sin—period." My son sees him as a selfish SOB. Their dad blames me for poisoning the kids. His lawyer even sent me a letter telling me that he felt like an outcast to his family ... "Duh! You left, were not driven out and in fact were asked to come back to work it out." He has yet to take responsibility for what he's done, nor has he apologized to the kids or anyone for that matter. The kids are not in any contact with him by their choice ... it's sad.

Mary Jane echoes the refrain that so many women heard from their departed husbands—"You poisoned the kids against me!" Even my ex-husband tried that *poor-me* tactic, and the "kids" that he was referring to were 27 and 29 years old—certainly old enough to make up their own minds. Like the husbands of many other SWAP participants, when he came face-to-face with the children's outrage, he fell back on the "I'm the victim here" defense.

The kids don't have to be adults, however, to recognize that their dad did something that really hurt their mom. Even very young children, or perhaps especially very young children, have well-established codes of right and wrong. Even if kids don't know the word, they know that the deed of adultery falls in the "wrong" category. But they are often caught in an uncomfortable place because as much as they might deem Daddy's actions as bad, they still love him and need him. They often become stuck in a loyalty bind, knowing how upset their mother is but still missing their dad. And seeing Dad quickly means having to get to know the very person whom children blame for all this mess, the girl-friend.

Forty-four-year-old Freya and her husband, Tim, had two small children when he left the marriage six years ago and moved in with his girlfriend. Freya says that both her 5-year-old son and 3-year-old daughter were profoundly affected.

The first summer after he left, he insisted on taking them on a two-week vacation with his lover to the cottage we'd formerly shared. This, of course, was very hard for my kids. After that vacation, my son told me he realized his father didn't love him, as he cried and related various things that the love-birds had done to my kids, and in front of them, over the holiday.

My son detests his stepmother and hates many of the things his father does and says but still desperately wants his father's affection and is deeply hurt by everything that continues to happen. My daughter went right off the deep end, and really it's only in the last year or two that she's started to recover. She obviously didn't understand what was going on in the beginning and was terribly afraid. She'd cling to me, hide, and have to be ripped off me when he'd take her for a visit.

Of course, some of the issues that the children of SWAP participants face are typical to all divorced families and not a function of the unusual circumstances surrounding wife aban-donment. There are three aspects, however, that are almost al-ways present in WAS that don't always exist in typical divorce scenarios: (1) the mother is traumatized and (2) there is a girl-friend already on the scene prior to the separation, hence (3) it is very difficult to develop a functional co-parenting relationship.

Robyn, whose kids were 3 and 8 at the time of the separation four years ago, illustrates:

> Kids do not want to pick sides, and although they are fully
> aware of what happened (unfortunately), it has had a big toll
> on them. Keeping the peace and keeping things calm have
> been what they want the most. That's not their jobs, but that
> was their take on the situation. Since my relationship with
> their father is still not very good, and horrible with his girl-
> friend, they have to deal almost on a weekly basis with
> issues and poor feelings.

Recovery from WAS is more complicated for those women who have children going back and forth between parents' houses. As much as it might be necessary for the ex-wives to put a buffer of distance between themselves and their former spouse in order to heal, they still have to be constantly in contact with him, either directly or through the kids. Many kids of divorce often know how to bisect themselves—"Shhh, don't tell mommy about daddy and don't tell daddy about mommy"—but the information seeps through when a parent asks, "Where did you go? What did you eat? Who was there?" or the child innocently recounts the events of his time with the other parent. Even the most mature and care-ful parents find that their kids often unwittingly become drawn into the painful drama that is unfolding between their parents.

What's Wrong with Mom?

Even in the best of times, it takes a lot of energy to be a good par-ent. We need patience, creativity, home-making skills, humor, self-discipline, a good nature and the trick of making paper flowers out of tissues and twist-ties. As much as we may love the job of parenting, there's no denying that it requires our spirit and attention. But when we've been hit by a truck and can hardly get our own teeth brushed, let alone fight with our 7-year-old to brush his, what a mom can provide often gets whittled down to the bare minimum. This causes the already suffering mother great grief. Forty-two year old Anita remembers the early days just following the revelation:

> "Things were dark, but the only thing I really remember was when I stopped parenting my children. It was a struggle to go to work everyday and I managed to go through the motions there, but the neglect of my children (making them meals, having food in the house, making sure they had clean laundry, doing fun 'kid' things with them) makes me the saddest when I look back at it all."

I take my hat off to those of you who had to keep it up for the sake of kids at home. I often thought, back when my husband left, that if it was so hard for me to cope, it must be a thousand times harder for mothers of young kids. There are many conflicting emotions on the part of mothers as they struggle to do the right thing for their kids while at the same time wishing they could tell the kids what a liar Daddy was and have them turn against him. Here are some thoughts from SWAP participants that illustrate this dilemma:

- "I wanted our kids to hate him (they have each struggled with this in their own way)."
- "It is so hard for me to try to stay neutral when I'd really like him to understand how much our kids are hurting."
- "The only persons with any dignity and self-respect through all this were our poor children."
- "The most difficult thing for me was balancing my hurt with my need to keep my children sane and without guilt."
- "At first I dumped on them a lot. I felt so needy. But they helped me see that this was straining my relationship with

them, and so we agreed that I'd dump on a therapist or
my brother."

- "I had a couple of wine-induced ballistic breakdowns in
  front of my children. I felt jealous of them when he would
  see them. At the same time I wanted them to have a father."

Although it's normal to give in occasionally to the temptation
to enlighten the kids about the reality of the situation, setting
them straight too brutally ends up hurting them. The best gift you
can give to your kids in this situation is to try not to draw them
into this. They are entitled to their childhoods, or, if they're young
adults, they are entitled to their lives. Of course, some younger
kids ask questions and try to comfort their moms—after all, it's
happening to them too! And teens and young adults often become
very much involved. But I'm suggesting that your job is to try to
not encourage that involvement and to respond to your kids'
needs, while looking toward appropriate adults, as much as possible, to attend to yours.

Forty-one year old Adrienne, who had a young son and baby
girl when her husband left, had to reach down deep inside to find
the courage to do the right thing for her son.

The day my husband told me he was leaving, my son started
to cry, and my husband suggested my son go with him, just
for the night. My son was four and I had never been apart
from him for a single night. I wanted to scream and hold on
to him for dear life, to not lose anything more than I was
already about to lose. A voice deep inside me told me I had
to put myself aside and do what was best for my son, and I
let him go. He stopped crying and left with my husband.

I will never forget seeing the two of them walk away
down the path to the car at that moment, knowing what it
meant. I felt nauseous and paralyzed, and I was alone with
my baby with no one to help (my family all lived on the
opposite coast). Somehow I had to pick her up and be a
mom. I did.

And so began a long new road of daily digging deep into my core to constantly differentiate decisions made out of anger from decisions made for the best interests of the children. That part has always been and will always be a struggle. For the most part I have, but it has never gotten easier.

Adrienne's courage that permitted her to put her children first is truly inspiring. Like her, many women said that it was the kids that forced them to function and that having kids required them to pull themselves together as soon as humanly possible. The pattern of daily life that children's schedules impose on a family naturally creates order out of chaos. And a mother will do things for her kids, like cooking a meal or straightening up the house, which she wouldn't bother to do for herself.

He Left Us Too!

In more typical divorce scenarios, the father/child bond sometimes gets stronger because the single-parent father may be doing much more direct childcare than he ever did when he was married. Making ponytails and preparing lunch boxes can enrich the connection between a dad and his child as they grow to know each other in a new way. Mothers play an important role in fostering that father/ child bond if they see that connection as valuable to the child and encourage it. In cases of WAS, however, two factors work against that happening: (1) the mother is in no frame of mind to do anything that might benefit her runaway ex, and (2) the father is phobic about contact with his former wife and wants to minimize it as much as possible. He avoids facing her anger or the possibility of a scene at the handover of the kids. The parents are typically enemies. As a result, father/child relationships often become tense and stilted, and children lose out.

Many SWAP participants wrote that their children had become far more distant from their fathers, even when he had been a great dad and his pre-separation connection with the kids had been profound. Post-WAS, however, the kids felt every bit as abandoned as their mom. There were a significant number of cut-offs, both on the part of kids who no longer wanted anything to do with their dads, and by dads who couldn't manage to keep connected to their kids. Many women rued the fact that their children's father did not adequately support the kids financially after he left. Mothers resented paying the full cost of college fees but did so for fear of compromising the child's education. The deterioration of the father/child bond is a tragedy because even if a man behaved badly toward his wife at the end of the marriage, his relationship with his kids needs to be salvaged if at all possible.

I want to highlight here three other special circumstances related to kids that were especially heartbreaking for SWAP participants. The first one is when husbands left wives who were pregnant or had just had a baby. There is a special kind of outrage reserved for men who participate in bringing a child into the world when they are already toying with the idea of leaving. Mothers who were pregnant at the point of abandonment were worried that the deep grief they experienced would affect the development of their unborn child. They also mourned the loss of the father in the life of the child and felt terribly guilty that they couldn't provide an optimal life for their child, even though it was not their fault. Thirty-six-year-old Carol, who was four months pregnant when her husband left, recounted this poignant memory:

> When they did the first ultra-sound and I found out Joshua was going to be a boy, I was so disappointed because I thought, "How will I take him to the men's room? I don't know how hockey equipment fits!" I thought to myself, "It's going to be a lonely world for me," but a daughter, I could understand. A son without a dad just broke my heart. And now I feel so guilty about feeling that instead of just rejoicing for my son. So that was probably one of the darkest moments.

The second special circumstance having to do with the effect on kids of WAS was when the former couple had adopted a child, which was the case with quite a few women in the study. Moms often feel super-protective of an adopted child who has already experienced a significant loss in his or her young life, and they really rue the fact that they couldn't prevent this child from experiencing a second major disruption. Bonnie's marriage had ended ten years earlier, but her voice still quivered when she told about her shock at this injustice done to her daughter:

> I was extremely focused on my daughter. As much as I have just expressed how hurt I was, if I go to the place about what he did to my daughter, it's way worse. Because I'm an adult and this kid had already been abandoned by two biological parents, taken from her country into our arms, and this was never what I wanted for her, and she was two— what an age to go through this.

Brianna and her husband were working their way through the challenging process of applying to adopt a second child and had just completed the home study when he left. The mother of a 3-year old, Brianna feared for the repercussions on her daughter:

> I experienced a tremendous amount of grief and guilt over somehow allowing this to happen to our daughter—the darkest thoughts were of what this would mean for her. She should have been assured of a better life after having been put up for adoption. She was a "crack" baby and her birth mother did not know the identity of the birth father. She will have to contend with that as well as the fact that her adoptive father walked out on her after having her less than two years. I feel she will ultimately blame herself for the timing one day.

That righteous anger about harm done to an innocent child

propels some women to assume a "mother tiger" stance, which gives the woman a focus for her outrage. It's a whole lot easier to fight for the rights of your child than it is to defend yourself in the face of your ex-husband's accusations of the wrongs done to him.

The third special circumstance regarding kids was when the woman did not have children herself but had participated in raising her husband's children, as their stepmother. When the marriage ends, the abandoned wife is often left in a "no woman's land," no longer having any formalized relationship with those kids. If the kids are young, they cannot be expected to go back and forth between mom's house, dad's house and step-mom's house, so she naturally loses out. If the kids are adults, they may opt to avoid conflict by not inviting the stepmother to events. It's hard enough to negotiate birthdays juggling a mom and a dad who are divorced—if they can eliminate the added complication of inviting the step-mom (who would then have to deal with her ex-husband's girlfriend), they understandably will. For these women, no longer having an easy family relationship with children and grandchildren is an incalculable loss.

Co-parenting in a War Zone

Those of us who work in the field of divorce know that the best predictor of healthy development for children of divorce is a low level of conflict between the parents. But how, exactly, do you manage *that* when the whole process begins with the lobbing of a hand grenade? Dr. Thomas H. Smith, a divorce mediator in Boulder, Colorado, wrote about how "a battle over custody" may contain metaphors similar to an actual battle in a war:

- The two divorcing parents correspond to the two enemies in war.
- Taking over the children corresponds to taking over territory.

- The decision on custody corresponds to the outcome of one of the battles of a war.
- Prejudicing the children against the other parent corresponds to war propaganda.
- Suffering of the children corresponds to damage to territory fought over in war.

I used a war metaphor, collateral damage, as the title to this chapter. It's defined as damage that is unintended or incidental to the intended outcome. No one wants to hurt the children in a divorce. It's hard to steer away from images of attack and retreat in the face of WAS, yet the job of raising a healthy child will force you to try to find a way to make a truce in that arena and function with neutrality.

Children derive their identity from both their parents, and as much as they may carry the physical characteristics of their parents, they also have both their mom's and their dad's personality traits. The way that you represent your ex to your kids tells them as much about you as it does about their father. And, although as kids they may not understand the extent of the wrong that he has done, one day they should be able to assess it correctly through adult eyes. But in the process, you don't want them to grow up resenting you for poisoning their dad to them.

To become mentally healthy adults, they need to come to terms with the failings of their parents as people, but as kids growing up, they benefit from a strong relationship with each of their parents. The paradox is that, to facilitate that relationship, you'll need to validate your child's connection with his father in spite of the fact that you may hate the man and have lost respect for his character. Nevertheless, you need to sit down and think long and hard about how to manage this very tricky part of your life and how to insure that, years from now, you'll feel proud of the decision you made.

The first step in this process is to cobble together an explanation as to why Daddy left that will permit your child to maintain a relationship with him. Believe me, I know that it's practically impossible to shield your child from the tsunami that hit you, but at least you can choose not to contribute to the damage. The explanation you come up with may sound bland, but it's better than pulling out the heavy artillery. As much as you'd love to say, "Daddy is a liar and a cheater and his girlfriend is a whore," for example, don't go there! On the other hand, you'd choke on an explanation like, "We just grew apart and decided to separate," so that's not recommended either.

I believe kids needs a minimum level of truth so they have something to grab on to. So although every fiber in your body may be screaming for you to use four-letter words in your explanation, perhaps it's prudent to say something like this: "Your dad has decided to end the marriage and he's moved out. He says that he's not been happy for a long time. I didn't know that—he hadn't told me till now—so I'm struggling to understand what happened. I may be a bit of mess while I'm figuring this all out, but I promise that I'll get it together as soon as possible. Oh, and you need to know that he's moved in with another woman."

Of course, by the time that you're reading this, you've already told your kids all sorts of things. It's never to late to put a cork in it, though, if what's been coming out of your mouth has needed editing. You can't take back what you've said, but you can clean up your act for the future.

There's no doubt that some fathers distance themselves from their children, and as much as it breaks your heart, there's little you can do about your ex-husband's choice in that. Just make sure that you don't use his contact with the kids as an opportunity to rant at him. If he has to run the gauntlet of your anger every time he comes to pick up your children, you'll unwittingly be damaging his relationship with them and making it more likely that he'll give up that connection.

If your ex-husband has made it clear that he's not interested in being much involved in the kids' lives, the best you can do there is to reinforce to your children that it was not because of them that Daddy left. Avoid saying that Daddy left "us." Although some runaway husbands *are* fleeing from the whole package, there's no doubt that the primary person they are leaving is the wife. And although it might paint him as more of a louse and make you feel better to lump the children in with you among the discarded, your kids will probably have a secret wish that Daddy cares enough to keep in touch. So it's best to clarify that Daddy left *you*, not them, and if he's not keeping in touch with them, it may be because he's afraid to face you. Avoid the temptation to use his poor showing with the kids as more proof to the world that he has behaved badly. What he did to you is bad enough. Try to keep your children out of it.

Creepy Dad

There's a special twist to the situation with older teens and adult kids. Like younger kids, they may be upset about the divorce of their parents and worried about their mom, but older kids are aware of the sexual nature of their dad's illicit liaison, and many report feeling very creeped out by it. They come face-to-face with their dad's excitement about a girlfriend who may be just a few years older than they are, and the passionate nature of it threatens them. Kids like to think of "Mom and Dad" as just parents—in most families the sexual side of that relationship is largely hidden. Now, suddenly, dad's wearing tight jeans and his eyes are all aglow. The kids can't avoid seeing him in a new and disturbing light, and they don't like it. They wonder what goes through his mind when he meets their friends; perhaps he's having sexual thoughts about them, too? As a result, they no longer trust him in the innocent way they did before, and that's a rupture that's hard to mend.

Teens and young adults, like 17-year-old Alexandra, whom we met earlier, who are at the stage in life of trying to establish their own long-term relationships, get thrown a monkey wrench when their fathers abandon their moms. They reason that if their parents' happy, secure marriage could fall to pieces in the blink of an

eye, how can they ever be sure that a future spouse won't have an
affair and walk out on them too? Some adult kids of WAS have
said that they've "sworn off men," "would never get married" or
"are afraid that their husbands will abandon them once they have
children." As difficult as it is these days for young adults to trust
in relationships, it's much harder when they feel they have no way
to protect against unanticipated abandonment.

The "No Drama!" Pledge

The best way you can help your kids through their recovery from
WAS is for you to get stronger yourself. As you are now cycling
through good days and bad in the Sun Shower Transformational
Stage, it's time to take the **"No Drama!"** pledge. That means, each
time something upsetting happens and you have a choice to either
pump up your outrage or cool it down, remember to say to yourself, "No Drama!" and choose the path of simplicity and stabil-
ity. Try to avoid interpreting every action of your ex through a
negative filter that causes you to define it in the worst possible
light. For example, if he gets your daughter an expensive present
for her birthday, rather than immediately getting mad and labeling it an effort to "buy off" the kids, permit the possibility that the
gift was given out of love. You'll be making the choice to leave the
drama behind and to reach for the light.

CHAPTER 14

The SWAP Girls'
Bag of Tricks

It was a cold but bright winter's morning some months after my husband left, and I was on my way to fetch my car from the repair shop. I'd been walking on the shady side of the street and crossed over to enjoy the sunshine. When I stepped up on the opposite curb, a realization hit me. Had my husband been with me, I would've had to stay on the shady side of the street; due to his medical problems, he couldn't take the sun. Enjoying the fragile warmth on my face, I mused about the fact that the moment was a metaphor for the transition that was taking place in my life. I'm crossing over from the shady to the sunny side again and can see many ways in which I have been freed up from daily sacrifices, large and small, that I routinely used to make on my husband's behalf.

In the **Early Spring Transformational Stage**, although the traces of winter and all you've suffered are still very present, new opportunities will start to bud as you open your heart to change. You've clung to life through the tsunami, survived the tornado, weathered the thunderstorm, endured the ice storm, kept going in spite of the fog, sheltered under an umbrella in the sun shower and now are starting to have hope. It's probably been at least a year since your life shape-shifted; more likely closer to two. This recovery takes time. By the time you reach Early Spring, you will no longer be obsessing as intensely, although you may still be thinking about "it" many times during the day. The acute pain

will largely have passed. You'll be eating again. You will be working on the sixth of the **Seven Steps for Moving Forward**: turning
your focus from the past to the future.

Perhaps, like me, you will start to recognize some of the positives associated with your husband's departure. Apart from the
obvious ones, like not having to cook dinner every night or being
free to paint the bedroom lavender, there are more subtle plusses
that become apparent. As you challenge yourself to manage your
life solo, you'll start to realize that you're more capable than you
thought. You may enjoy the feeling of being the captain of your
own ship. Forty-one year old Georgia, who told the story in an
earlier chapter about learning to love the inscribed watch her husband had given her, lyrically describes a pivotal moment similar
to the one in which I crossed over to the sunny side:

> One day as I sat in a rocking chair at dusk in the springtime
> not long after he'd left, I noticed something in the air that
> almost took my breath away. My kids were playing quietly
> and no one was crying (between the three of us, someone
> usually was at that time). I could hear the birds outside. I
> identified the feeling as the sound of a house where everyone
> in it loved each other. A beautiful peace had descended on
> our home. It was only at that moment I realized how much
> I'd internalized my husband's dislike for me, and how long it
> had been there without me consciously recognizing it. I had
> felt inherently unlikable for longer than I could remember
> and had never realized that the feeling was coming from
> him. At that same moment I also knew how fiercely I would
> protect that harmony in my house from then on. Seven years
> later, I still do.

It's only when something is over and you can look at it from
a different vantage point that you can truly assess how it has been
affecting you. When Georgia's husband left, she was finally able
to put her finger on what that had been nagging at her for so
long—feeling unlikable in his eyes. Another study participant,

Holly, had a pleasant surprise when she realized that her migraines walked out the door along with her husband: "I realized that my body knew something before my head and my heart did. I discovered that it would be healthier for me with him gone."

Tricks of the Betrayed

In this chapter, I'm putting on my postman hat. I'm going to deliver messages directly to you from those who have gone through WAS and want to tell you what they've learned. I want to share with you the *SWAP Girls' Bag of Tricks*—the answers on the questionnaire to my query about what tricks women had used to get through the hard times.

Some of the tricks suggested apply to the early days post-revelation, while others relate more to later on in the process of recovery. No matter. We know that recovery is a "two-steps forward/one-step-back" process, so these suggestions are valuable at any stage. Many of the women who participated in the study said that it made them feel good to be able to help someone else. Following our discussion of tricks, we'll segue right into a discussion of the advice that the study participants had to offer. This chapter will be a veritable vitamin B-12 shot for you, speeding you along your way to your new life with maybe a laugh or two *en route*. Here's a list of brilliant tricks for recovery from a bunch of very resourceful women.

The SWAP Girls' Bag of Tricks!

- I feigned happiness—though I felt like a total fake.
- I arranged salsa dance classes for my daughter and me.
- I read Marianne Williamson's book, *Everyday Grace*.
- I scuba dove.
- I arranged a woman's writing group, doing the *Artist's Way* together, which was a fabulous release.

- I engaged in what I call "movie therapy" and watched countless "chick flicks."
- To be honest, having a brief fling with a neighbor's contractor helped me quite a bit.
- I had a song, "Tubthumping" by Chumbawumba—"I get knocked down and I get up again."
- A friend sent a HAPPY journal where I would write one thing a day that made life worth living.
- I talked to my lapdog a lot.
- I had my first one night stand that turned into a two-and-a-half-year relationship [laugh].
- I actually worked at my friendships, making sure I was a better friend than I used to be.
- One big trick that helped me was really focusing on what I wanted, looking at what made me happy and how I could achieve that.
- Well, one thing is never to go to bed ugly! Typically, you get up, look in the mirror at a tear-stained face, uncombed hair and burlap nightie and say, "No wonder he left me!!" Buy yourself some really nice, pretty jammies. Have a bath with scented oils. Do your hair, put on a little makeup and admire your reflection before you go to bed! Stretch out in the bed, take it all, and feel sorry for all the guys who'll never see your loveliness.
- Plan a trip. Doesn't have to be a big one, but keep planning things you're going to look forward to.
- Laugh at it, because in the end, it's all so ridiculous, isn't it?
- I would just watch *Seinfeld*.
- I read a lot of detective books.
- I started a Master's of Social Work program a week after my husband moved out. My classmates practiced their skills on me.
- I power walked a lot! I went so far as to borrow my neighbor's dog to feel that sense of control. Then I got a German shepherd—he taught me that what he needed was a calm but confident pack leader. I try to draw on that as much as I can.

- Bowling!
- I skied every chance I could—it was my salvation. I cried, sobbed, while I skied and the tears would be frozen on my face but I told myself to just keep going. Put one foot in front of the other and just keep going.
- Oddly enough, one of the best things I did was join a martial arts class.
- I prayed a lot, found faith. When it all got absolutely too much, sometimes I would just close my eyes, put my head on the side and pretend that I was leaning on God's shoulder and try to just imagine that he was taking all the worries for a few minutes.
- I live in the present.
- For the first time in my life I asked for help and was not only a helper.
- The phone was my friend and I used it shamelessly.
- I began serious meditation and yoga.
- I look at nature, at the little bird in my backyard, or the flower, a butterfly.
- I do an exercise where I breathe in all of the pain and hurt and then exhale love, forgiveness and compassion.
- Affirmations helped.
- I forced myself to think positively, even when I had to deal with him—I would force myself to be civil and eventually it started to come naturally.
- Laugh, laugh, laugh!
- I had to break my days down into small periods and concentrate on just getting through those times.
- Each night when I went to bed I said, "God, I leave it in your hands tonight, I'm going to sleep."
- Fake it till you make it, keep positive, lots of other mantras from my online support group.
- My motto was "This too shall pass."
- A trick I got from another friend is to be the star of your own little TV show. Visualize yourself moving bravely forward, like Mary Tyler Moore or (insert your favorite screen

heroine here), and create your own happy endings, or glamorize the sad ones. It gives you some distance.

- I've found writing in a journal to be very therapeutic.
- Accepted any invitation I received.
- I found Facebook and within a week of joining I was in touch with friends from my last job, college friends and even high school friends, not to mention current ones.
- I took my wedding band and made it into a toe ring and every time I felt upset I would squash my foot.
- Whenever I was feeling "too low for zero," I would try and think of something I could do for someone else.
- I read the book *On Your Own Again* and found it very useful.
- I read the book *The Language of Letting Go* by Melody Beattie.
- The first thing I did was join a hiking and adventure club.
- I renovated houses.
- I listened to funk, to Aretha Franklin, James Brown, tons of Nikka Costa and to old cocktail lounge music.
- I learned to drive.
- I got my hair cut very short.
- I joined Toastmasters.
- I started going to workshops at Home Depot to add to my home maintenance skills.
- In the end what was the most healing was getting pregnant.
- I compete in performance events with my dogs.
- I now do yoga once a week. I love it! I started dancing. I love it!!
- I decided in June to study for my MCAT exams and try to go back to medical school.
- I sing in two choirs and play the piano at a bunch of seniors' homes.
- I accepted an invitation to join a group of co-workers who had a theater subscription because I'd always liked live theater.

• My sense of humor was vital to my recovery. I remember soon after his disclosure, I took a book out of the library called *I Love You, Let's Work It Out*. Right after I took out that book, my husband moved out. So I walked back to our small town library. *I Love You, Let's Work it Out* went into the return slot and I took out *If You're Leaving Me, Put it in Writing*. This struck me as hilarious!

Okay. I admit it. Writing the **SWAP Girls' Bag of Tricks!** made *me* cry. I thought about all the struggle and courage it took for all of us to keep trying to be strong and healthy and I burst into tears. You all are so terrific! Keep fighting!

So what tricks did I have? Like so many of you, I started going to the gym like my life depended on it. Pounding the treadmill with rock music blaring through my headphones felt good, in spite of the fact that I often had to give myself a kick in the behind to get there because my soul was in a state of mortal agony. I'd lost a lost of weight and with all that working out, I got into shape and that felt good, too. But that was secondary—it was the physical release that drove me.

Initially, crossword and jigsaw puzzles helped occupy my mind during those long, silent evenings. But then, I did something unexpected. For the first time in my life, I was free and unencumbered and what did I do? I got an eight-week-old puppy. And not any calm cheerful dog, like a lab or a golden—I got myself a Jack Russell mix. If you know dogs, you know that Jack Russells are craaaaazy! They're really smart and wildly funny, but they have endless energy. Shortly after I got Chloe, I was talking with my hairdresser, who is also a yoga instructor and a very spiritual person, about my hare-brained decision to tie myself down. She said we get dogs and cats because of "an excess of love." We have all this love to give and need someone to be around to receive it.

So once Chloe entered my life, things took a turn for the better. I was busy training and walking her, which got me integrated into my neighborhood in a way that I'd never been before. Everyone knew Chloe and so everyone knew me. I entered into the secret society of dog owners who meet in the park every night at nine to chat while we watch the canines frolic. But mostly I love her a lot and she makes me smile.

But the really *out of left field* thing that I did was to join a women's *a capella* barbershop chorus. I have a terrible voice and my family would always make jokes whenever I open my mouth. If anyone had told me six months earlier that I'd be standing on risers in a church basement every Wednesday night singing barbershop, I would never have believed it. But the chorus turned out to be one of the most meaningful things I've ever done.

The very first rehearsal I attended, the chorus was given a new song to learn. It's called "There Goes My Heart" and tells the story of a woman whose beloved husband suddenly leaves her and moves in with his girlfriend. I'm not kidding. I thought, "Okay, well, I'm *outta* here. No way am I going to sing this song." But I stood up there on the risers week after week, and when I'd start crying, someone would make a joke or squeeze my hand and I just kept on singing. I decided that when I'd sung that song a hundred times, I'd be cured. So I threw my heart and soul into it and got really expressive, and now, of course, singing the song no longer hurts (much).

The chorus meets every week, summer and winter, and during that two-and-a-half-hour period, I need to forget about myself completely in order to blend with the others. Every woman there has her own problems, so I can't mope around (if I can help it) because it's a downer for the others. But when we start singing, magic happens. There's nothing more therapeutic than making music. And, by the way, my voice is improving!

So, unlike some of the women quoted in the *SWAP Girls' Bag of Tricks!*, most of us can't get pregnant, renovate houses or go back to school for our medical degree, but we can all sing, dance, paint, read, walk, bowl and listen to cocktail lounge music, or whatever it is that means that you're alive and still kicking, and no one can hold you down!

Dear Abby (and Betty and Susan and Carol)

The list above was in answer to a question about what tricks women used. In this section, SWAP participants who have walked in your shoes and are a little farther down the road will provide suggestions of a more profound nature—the truths they learned about life and how to live it. Although these thoughts will help you through this crisis, they are applicable to any other time in your life when you are suffering.

The first stream of advice is along the lines of "time will heal." This is something we all know theoretically, but it's hard to hold on to when your heart is really hurting. If you can get on top of the idea that life holds unknowable potential and that the pain of suffering always dims as time passes, then your sadness will not be tinged with desperation. If you choose to believe that you will ALWAYS be miserable and you'll NEVER have a happy day again in your life, you're heading in the wrong direction. When you're really struggling, remind yourself, "It *feels* like my life will never get better, but some part of me *knows* that time will heal." Here are some messages from SWAP participants to encourage you:

- "Hold on. DO NOT let go of life! Remember—it feels like a tsunami now but you WILL survive, and one day you might even walk the same beach and bless the waters for making you stronger."
- "Even though people will tell you that you will recover and you'll think, 'You're full of crap, please leave me alone, I want to wallow in my pain,' you will get better and you'll be stronger for it. There is a better life for you in your future."
- "Fasten your seatbelt because it's going to be a rough ride for at least the first year. Don't expect a linear progression in terms of things 'getting better.' The sense of loss and disorientation continues for a long time and disappears slowly."
- "It is a horrible, dark and scary tunnel, but go through it, feel it all fully and totally. There is light at the end. I promise. Meet your new, emerging self coming out as you go. You

will be amazed at what you will become. Be extra kind and loving and generous to your self."

A sub-clause to the "this too shall pass" advice is the suggestion to take the time you need to heal. We've touched on this before, but it's worth repeating that you shouldn't feel like a failure because you haven't recovered as quickly as others expect you to. Here we remember the maxim that there's no way around it—you have to go through it. When you think of the healing metaphor, if you've cut your hand, your body will take some time to repair. There is a process it must go through to seal off the damaged blood vessels and restore the torn tissue. Much as you might want it to be better tomorrow, it must take the time it needs.

You can facilitate that process by keeping the wound clean, getting enough rest and eating properly, but there remains a minimum amount of time that's immutable—beyond your control. However, you should notice progress over time—the skin becoming less red and tender, a scab forming. If weeks pass and your hand is not improving, it's time to seek professional help. Something might be interfering with the body's natural recuperative process. Stretching this metaphor to apply to our situation, if you find that after a year, you're still very much in crisis, it's time to seek some counseling with a therapist who understands Wife Abandonment Syndrome.

Some women who have been through it warn against letting this experience become an excuse for ongoing self-pity. Several repeated the "living well is the best revenge" motto and wish to encourage you to be the best human being you can be—not for anyone else but for yourself. Here are their voices:

- "Your revenge is living the best of lives. And please DO NOT FEEL SORRY for YOURSELF. GET A LIFE!"
- "Take the high road. It makes everything simpler."
- "Try not to sink into despair, but work toward making a better life for yourself. Try to believe in light and love instead of becoming bitter—this is most important."

- "You have to not let it consume you! I would make lists some days of all the great aspects of my life, i.e., children, great friends, family, health, etc., and when I was feeling mad or sad or bad I would refer to these positive aspects of my life and try to stay focused on them."
- "Get over it as soon as you can. No man is worth tears and heartbreak. Make a concerted effort to be happy; life is so good, even alone."

When I was really struggling, those were the kinds of messages that helped me the most. I felt that being pitiful was not the way I wanted to live my life and would tell myself to "pour some steel into my spine," suck it up and get tougher. That image of strengthening my spine helped, particularly when I had to meet with my ex-husband face-to-face in the legal process of divorce. I would also tell myself to reach down into my gut and grab some courage (pretty gross, huh?). I used that image also as a way of encouraging myself not to indulge in becoming a whiner. I always had in mind that even though what was done to me by my ex-husband was really rotten, it pales in comparison to the unspeakable evil and injustices perpetrated throughout the world on a daily basis. Maintaining that perspective helped.

Finally, in the unadulterated advice column, SWAP women have one other message they want to transmit: Believe in yourself! Remember who you are, remember what you're worth, acknowledge that others love you, cut yourself some slack for not having been perfect, but know that you didn't deserve how you were treated. You must not use this as an opportunity to punish yourself; you need to treat yourself with love. Here's what they said:

- "Keep your self-esteem; this was NOT your fault, and there was nothing you could have done to prevent it. Do not beat yourself up because this is not about you."
- "Be strong! Believe in yourself no matter what!"
- "Take care of yourself! Discover who you have been created to be."

- "Believe that you are not a bad person, that we all try to our best and we all deserve to be alive and have a good life."
- "I think the most important thing is to trust what you're feeling about what's happening. Trusting yourself is the first step back toward solid ground."

I second all that excellent advice and encourage you to listen to these wise women. Their counsel may seem hard to put into practice at this point, but it is priceless and will lead you in the direction you really need to go—toward acceptance and growth.

CHAPTER 15

Turning Points

I've always said that there is good and bad in every situation, but it takes women subjected to WAS a long time to be able to look past the veil of pain in order to see the positives that resulted from their husband leaving. Some never get there, most are able to name some good things that came from it, but a surprising number report that the crisis of abandonment spurred them on to do things that they never would have accomplished from the comfort or restrictions of the marriage. The positives reported for abandoned wives fall largely into four categories:

1   They are liberated from their husband's negativity.
2   They learned that they are competent and independent.
3   They love the sense of freedom.
4   They headed off in new directions that would have been unthinkable before.

Many women didn't realize the extent to which they had been tiptoeing around their husband's moods till he left. They'd grown used to his being "a grump" in social situations or with their family, coping with the tension caused by his disapproval or criticism—as one woman wrote, he "sucked the fun out of a lot of things." While married, dealing with that negativity was just "a given," but it sure was a relief when the marriage ended and the wife recognized that she no longer had to manage that black cloud. Another SWAP participant wrote: "After a year, I realized how unhappy I'd been, how draining my husband was of my energy, without giving back to me. I felt like a huge weight was removed."

Several women wrote that they were happy that their children no longer had to deal with Dad's irritability on a daily basis and that, once the *sturm und drang* of the Thunderstorm Stage had lifted, the mood in the house was just more fun. Forty-six-year-old Lucy, married nineteen years, contributed: "My oldest daughter came home from university recently and brought a friend along. They stayed for five days. It was a peaceful, laughing, fun visit that would never have been possible if he were still here. It took almost two years before I was able to marvel at the peace in our home."

Some of the terror that women initially experienced when their husbands left stemmed from feeling that they couldn't manage all the complex tasks that are required to run one's life. Some had never balanced a checkbook, negotiated a lease with a landlord or had the oil changed in the car, for example, and they assumed that those jobs were beyond their capabilities. Since runaway husbands are typically not disposed to help out their ex-wives, the women were suddenly faced with a bunch of tasks that were brand new to them. Unless they had a solicitous relative or friend, they had to pick up the ball quickly and run with it alone.

Most soon learned that these jobs are not rocket science, and they could not only master them, but perhaps make better choices than their former husband did. Terri, 40 years old with three kids, was delighted at her ingenuity when she "replaced the extension cord that never fit the plug for the lawn mower and always slipped off while I would be cutting the lawn. It never occurred to me that I could do that before!" Women, like myself, who had never in their lives lived alone came to enjoy the simplicity of getting things done without having constantly to negotiate the terms.

You build your self-esteem when you accomplish something that you didn't think you could. I love the maxim, "Your reach should exceed your grasp." That means that you should challenge yourself to do things beyond your current skill set because pushing your limits makes you grow. When you find yourself suddenly alone, you're forced to rise to the occasion of rebuilding your life. In the end, you'll feel proud. We've been to the edge of the precipice, looked down into the abyss and stepped back into the light, changed. We've learned something about ourselves that no one can take away—we're fighters for our lives, and we're proud of our strength.

The other positive sentiment frequently expressed by women in the **Early Spring Transformational Stage** and onward was the pure enjoyment of their freedom. Most said they wouldn't trade being in a relationship for all that unadulterated freedom, but since it was thrust upon them, they reveled in it nevertheless. Leah, who volunteered for SWAP in spite of the fact that her marriage ended more than a decade before, has the perspective of time to analyze the changes in her life:

> I'm exactly who I'm supposed to be whether anybody likes
> it or not! That's the fun part! I was looking at my three-year-
> old granddaughter, Rebecca, being exactly who she is and
> thinking, "She's not attached to anything and she's free and
> wild and it's wonderful." That's what I feel like. I do what
> I please, if I don't like something, I'll say it. A lot of free-
> dom—that part's nice.

Leah went on to contrast how stress-free it is to travel with friends compared to when she used to travel with her husband: "When you travel with women, we'd make a wrong turn, and say, 'Whoops, we went the wrong way! We're two hours further away now.' Then we'd laugh and say, 'Oh, well, let's have a coffee'!"

Leah describes her pleasure in the sense of autonomy that eludes so many wives who are knee-jerk pleasers. We women are talented at taking care of everyone's needs but our own. Once there's no one else around, we slowly start to be able to hear our own quiet internal voice that we'd previously ignored. The voice is whispering to us that it's not a sin to take care of ourselves as well as we take care of others.

Being alone forces us to become more independently minded. With no one else to share the burden, we have to take responsibility for our own decisions. This includes large decisions about where to live, which lawyer to hire and whether to replace the old car, and smaller ones about which restaurant to choose and where to go on vacation. Plus it gets women out of the adolescent position of having to sneak around in order to avoid a husband's irritation. I can't tell you how many women wrote that they loved being able to buy whatever they wanted without needing to justify the purchase to anyone!

We'll be talking about the final positive outcome listed by SWAP participants, the fact that they headed off in new and unanticipated directions, a bit later.

Stepping out of the Box

That time I told about when I crossed over to the sunny side of the street would count as one of the mini turning points in my recovery. A turning point is a moment in life at which a decisive change occurs. It is sometimes the result of an event—for example, you get conclusive proof that your husband was having an affair—or it may come through a thought process in which the scales fall from your eyes and you suddenly view things differently. Turning points may be momentous (learning about the affair) or mini (realizing that I was free to walk in the sun). But even the mini-turnings can make a big difference and contribute to recovery.

Pina's turning point took place when the former event occurred—she stumbled upon proof that her husband had been having an affair. She'd found his journal and couldn't resist reading it. Suddenly she had an explanation for the incomprehensible way he'd left the marriage:

In this book was everything he'd left out. He'd lied about all the reasons for his leaving. He was madly in love with another woman, whom he'd been seeing before our marriage ended. This explained his manner and his mania. It was the weirdest moment—like looking at a puzzle with pieces scattered helter-skelter and suddenly seeing them all come together. I felt my feet hit the ground that day, after two months of falling. It was devastating to read, but it also saved my life. I found out that I wasn't crazy.

Marcy describes another kind of turning point, one that I think would do each of us a huge bit of good if we ever get the chance to replicate it. This turning point came two years after her husband left and was made possible by the encouragement of her new, very understanding boyfriend:

One day, I was crying for the umpteenth time and I blurted out, while he held me, "I've always hated those dishes!" (the ones my ex had bought). My boyfriend took me outside to the back patio and told me I could smash them all, but I had to explain why, and what I was angry about. Then he gave me a hammer and handed me the twelve dishes, one by one. It was the first time I could say out loud I was angry, and the first time anyone ever wanted to listen to that anger. It was a hugely pivotal moment. AND I got rid of the ugly dishes!

What Marcy is describing is a doubly cathartic experience. Her boyfriend not only encouraged her to let loose all the pent-up anger she felt inside but also insisted that she put those feelings into words. Even without the benefit of a hammer, a patio and twelve ugly dishes, we can and need to find ways to get those feelings out. Often that can be done through acts of self-expression, like journaling, dancing or painting, or through working it out in the gym or kick-boxing class, as we've talked about. And many women credit the kinds of activities where they step out of the

box as leading to a new way of thinking. Danita was ready to
move on and that's why she ventured out of her comfort zone and
did something uncharacteristic. What she did is an example of a
mini-turning that helped her have hope:

> One Friday evening, I decided to take my 6-year-old daugh-
> ter to a local ski hill. I hadn't skied in thirty years and I hate
> winter, but there was little else to do, so we rented skis,
> strapped them on and glided down a hill. The air was crisp,
> the sky was dark and dappled with stars, and the snow was
> perfect. I hadn't laughed so hard in ages and I felt like I was
> really living. I got my courage back. I remember saying a
> prayer of thanks to God for drawing me to the ski hill and
> making me appreciate the life that I had. I got my groove
> back on that hill.

Another example of a turning point that came out of a realization happened to Heather when she was rushed to the hospital
with a gall bladder attack. Her kids were out of town, as was her
doctor, and through the pain, both physical and emotional, she
was forced to accept the fact that she could no longer depend on
her husband, who had recently left:

> I found myself in the hospital, all alone. My husband knew I
> was there and did not even call me, let alone come to be with
> me. This was four months after he left, and I realized he just
> didn't care about me, never mind love me, and that I was
> going to have to fend for myself from now on. It was revela-
> tory, and I came home from the hospital more accepting and
> ready to face what life has brought me.

And finally, Anita's answer to the question about turning
points will give us all hope. If this could happen to her, it can
happen to you:

I had been thinking of him every single day, sometimes every-waking-moment-of-every-single-day, and felt sorry that I was using my energy with those kinds of thoughts and anxious fears. Then, one day, when I was thinking of him, I realized, "Oh my gosh! ... I don't think I thought of him yesterday. I don't think I thought of him yesterday! I don't think I thought of him yesterday!!" And so, after two years of constantly thinking of him, I began the happy prospect of not doing that anymore. It was the beginning of the end of allowing my world to be possessed by him. It was, as people had previously told me "that God would eventually open a door," and when I looked up and saw the door was open, boy, did I run through it!

Anita's life had geared up and was ready for change. She saw opportunity and jumped at the chance. With her story of suddenly becoming aware that she'd moved on as a springboard, we will move on too from the **Early Spring Transformational Stage** to the next step, **Warm Summer Day.** Here we will see wondrous things—how some SWAP participants are truly happy about the redefinition of their lives post–Wife Abandonment Syndrome.

CHAPTER 16

Embracing Change

My friend Lynn came to visit me from California with her beau, Hugh, about eight months after my husband left. Hugh was quite interested in what had happened, and we spent a lot of time talking about it. Whenever I would go back to chewing on the old topic of my husband and his motivations, Hugh would quietly say to me, "It's not about him; it's about you." In the course of that weekend, he repeated that many times and each time he did, it would stop me and redirect my thinking. Hearing it just once wouldn't have been enough, but hearing it over and over was almost hypnotic and really made an impression on me. Little by little, the message got through—*he* doesn't matter any more. It's about *me*—my healing, my growth and what *I'm* going to do with my life.

Inspiration and encouragement are the centerpiece of this chapter in which you will learn more about how you can get to know the *New Me*! You may have a ways to go till you are completely over it, but you are learning to become a fighter for your happiness as you enter the **Warm Summer Day Transformational Stage.** By now, I hope that you have largely succeeded in mastering the sixth of the **Seven Steps for Moving Forward,** turning your attention from the past to the future, and are getting into the mind frame that will permit the seventh step—celebrating your new life as a single person.

One of the hardest parts of recovering is accepting the fact that you are single. You're not part of a couple; you are alone. You may be kept busy with your work, friends and family, but at the end of the day you get into bed alone. And being single is loaded. In our youth, we long to be part of a couple, and once we are, doesn't it feel secure to check that box on the form—married? So, it sometimes takes a while and often comes as a surprise when we get to the point of truly enjoying our solitude. That's not to say that we might not prefer to still be married, but we can often evolve to appreciate the pleasure of being alone.

I'm making a distinction here between being independent (able to stand on your own two feet and deal with the landlord when the roof leaks) and time spent with no one else around. At first, women who are filled with a lot of anxiety and worry try to avoid being alone at all costs, assuming that alone equals lonely. But eventually, many recognize that not only is life just fine on their own, but there's a special grace in enjoying solo time. Once they've learned to relish that, the anxiety and a lot of the fear melt away. After all, to be able to enjoy your own company, you must like yourself! So at the final stages of your recovery, open your mind to the realization that it's possible to be happy being alone. Because "It's not about him; it's about you."

The Paradox of Growth from Trauma

When I was in social work school, I learned that times of crisis provide an unexpected opportunity for growth. People are willing to try just about anything to reduce suffering and so are far more open to new ideas. Although we tend to think of traumatic events as uniformly negative, the potential for positives is evident when we think of the accomplishments of people like Christopher Reeves, Rick Hansen and Terry Fox. These are trauma survivors whose losses produced valuable gains that resulted from their struggle to cope, not from the trauma itself. University of North

Carolina researchers Lawrence Calhoun and Richard Tedeschi write about this paradox in their book, *Facilitating Posttraumatic Growth*. They define post-traumatic growth as "positive change that the individual experiences as a result of the struggle with a traumatic event." They suggest that individuals report growth primarily in three domains: change in relationships with others, change in the sense of self and change in philosophy of life.

Thirty-eight-year-old Jane, the architect from Tucson we heard from in an earlier chapter, provides a perfect example of how having experienced Wife Abandonment Syndrome changed her along all three dimensions:

> I'm grateful for having experienced pain at that level because it made me a more empathetic person. About a year after my husband left, there was a mine cave-in in Virginia and three miners were trapped. The wife of one of the men was interviewed and talked about those hours of anguish of waiting to hear. When I heard it, I got it! I know what a minute of anguish feels like, so when she said it was two hours, I understood what two hours of anguish feels like. It just touched me and I realized that if I could stay open to it, I now had the ability to really relate and not just intellectually say "That must be sad" but to actually feel it.
>
> It was through that pain that I feel plugged into the world and to other people in a profoundly different way. It's a different form of existence, and I wouldn't go back for a minute. My values have become really defined. I know what's important to me now and I speak up. I can bring things to consciousness that I couldn't before. I said to my therapist I'm so grateful to her because I feel like I've been reborn. I'm more "me" than I've ever been. I see things and understand things—it's a different level of consciousness.
>
> One of the people I've really admired during this period is Lance Armstrong—I feel like some of my feelings are like those of cancer survivors. I don't take things for granted now. My life is sort of settling back into a nice kind of

groove, but it's not going back to what it was. It changed me. I was on that road but I don't know I would've gotten here without this and I feel awake.

Jane fits the three criteria for posttraumatic growth to a tee. She describes a change in her relationship with others, now really getting it when people talk about their suffering. She talks about a change in her sense of self, feeling awake to the point of using the word "reborn." And there's been a profound change in her philosophy of life, knowing what's important to her and, like a cancer survivor, not taking things for granted. You may not have experienced an epiphany like Jane did and your realizations may be filtering through in dribs and drabs, but don't feel badly if you have not yet attained a radically new level of consciousness. For most, the process is layered and the result is cumulative. Change takes place slowly, and you're only aware that you're different in small increments. And remember, "It's not about him; it's about you."

Professional Help

Jane mentioned her therapist and how she feels thankful to her for her help. Certainly many, if not most, women who have suffered through WAS have sought the help of a counselor, with varying results. We talked about how different WAS is from a typical divorce, and some therapists are just not tuned in to that difference. They may assume that you were burying your head in the sand and that the warning signs were there all along. They may be blown away by the ferociousness of your pain and grief and start to push you toward recovery too soon. They may be convinced that your interminable sobbing is pathological and results from early losses in your childhood. Although that may be true (your childhood experiences certainly affect how you will react to adult hurts), the mere fact that you're in really rough shape does not necessarily indicate the presence of underlying emotional problems.

A number of women found that talking with the therapist wasn't much different than talking with a friend. A few were dismayed when their therapist's eyes filled with tears as they were telling their story. Mostly, women appreciated a therapist who believed them and provided insight into the process. Quite a few were deeply relieved when the therapist suggested that the ex-husband probably had psychological problems—narcissistic or sociopathic tendencies.

Priscilla describes her psychiatrist's approach, which is very much in tune with her needs:

> My psychiatrist is totally understanding. He's there for me
> 100%. Hard to believe a male can be so empathetic! He accepts my grief, supports my feelings and empathizes with my
> loss. He's non-directive and helps me find the answers in
> myself; he is consultative in his approach and helped me get
> a reduced workload. He assures me I am a good person
> and that the main fault lies in my husband's psychological
> makeup. Most importantly, he is an objective listener.

Sounds like Priscilla's psychiatrist is a gem! Jane also lucked out in being able to find just the right person for her after a false start:

> I started seeing a therapist and that was definitely helpful
> but eventually I saw a second therapist who turned my life
> around. I think she was very knowledgeable. I can remember
> a session early on in which she identified his narcissism. It
> really was the key for me. The first therapist was a lovely
> person in many ways, but in the first session she said, "We
> really need to discuss why you didn't see this coming"—not
> understanding that I was dealing with someone who was
> not normal and how that shifts everything. I'm really, really,
> really grateful for that second therapist because, along with

identifying the narcissism of my husband, she also pointed out that my mom's a narcissist too. It's just like the dominoes fell into place and all of a sudden a whole spectrum of feelings started to make sense.

Because Wife Abandonment Syndrome triggers a clinical depression in probably all women, antidepressants are often prescribed by doctors or suggested by therapists. I know that many people are reluctant to go that route, feeling that it betrays a weakness or fearing that they will become dependent on pills. In my experience as a therapist, a good number of depressed people who take medication in spite of their hesitation feel better as a result. They are more in control of their emotions and able to function more normally. Although some have trouble with side effects, like headaches or sleepiness, and others find that the meds just don't help, if your doctor prescribes them, I believe that it's worth a trial to see if you're one of the lucky ones who will get symptom relief.

Additionally, many women wrote about having found tremendous support from joining divorce recovery groups. Groups are powerful because they break the isolation so you don't feel like the only one to whom this has happened. When you get together with others going through similar experiences, you can encourage each other and share strategies for navigating all the complex systems involved in separating two lives. And the guidance of the group leader keeps the atmosphere constructive. Shauna, 62 years old, wrote: "I've met some wonderful counselors through my Divorce Recovery classes, and they have continued to stay in contact with me. I exchange weekly emails with them and when I see them, it's like seeing family. They really helped me put my pieces back together and now I'm standing much steadier."

Ideally, the group leaders will help participants remember that "It's not about him; it's about you."

The Gift of Clarity

When all is said and done, recovering from WAS is really about
the extent to which you will permit yourself to accept change.
Like the first of AA's twelve steps, admitting that we are powerless is the hardest step of all. All the thinking and trying to understand, strategizing and struggling, is about the very human need
to have some control over our lives. But something has happened,
like a tsunami on a sunny day, that we couldn't foresee and try as
we might, we can't undo. An unanticipated divorce means that a
lot of concrete things will change (you may need to find a job,
move to a new apartment or share your kids with your ex and his
girlfriend), but the biggest change of all takes place *inside* your
head—accepting that your future will not be as you planned.
Those who have learned from past experience to expect the unexpected will be find it easier to retool and move on. Those who
have never experienced major change in their lives or are lost if the
future doesn't conform to a predetermined plan, have a harder
time making the necessary changes.

It would be ideal if we could accept what life presented to us
and learn from it, but we keep trying to control things. That belief that we actually have much power over our lives is an illu-
sion—you really never know what the future will bring. So in the
face of having been forced by life's events (or your husband's
midlife crisis) to give up so much, part of the process of recovery
requires you to give up even more—voluntarily.

Give up the vision of your future with your husband. Give up
the prospect of enjoying your grandchildren together with him or
traveling when you both retire. Give up the pride in not being a
divorce statistic. Give up the easy companionship of having someone who's known you for decades—the pleasure of reminiscing
with him about happy or funny times in the past. Give up what
you'd hoped and expected your future to be like. Just give it all up
because you don't have any choice anyway. Just let it go!

But then, turn your vision to the parts of your future that *are*
in your hands—the one you now have the challenge to create. Pic-

ture yourself doing things that you enjoy with friends and family who love you. Accept that there are many kinds of love and that the love of a partner, although primary, is just one of them. Know that time will heal and the day will come when you will feel better. Bask in the pride of all you've accomplished and if you feel you haven't done enough of note, remember that it's never too late to do something courageous. Be proud of your struggle not to sink into self-pity or make the end of your marriage into a war medal you wear for all the world to see. And, most important, learn to love yourself and not to fear your time alone. After all, this is *your* life—not the fantasy life you expected to live. This is your real life—embrace it and show the world your stuff!

On this topic of adjusting to rapid change, Genevieve wrote:

> One thing I have come to realize four years later. Clarity. When my former life partner left so suddenly and I was in such shock, I had to very quickly regroup, redefine, and "re-" so many things! But in some ways, it was almost easier, I think, than the painful process so many people go through of years of marital deterioration and breakdown—the arguments, accusations, confusion and ugliness. OK—I was hit hard and I was hit well—but as a result, my priorities became so vividly clear. I am only now realizing what a gift I was given—the gift of clarity. Though I don't know how many others out there have had the same feeling, I thought that this insight might be of use to those in the midst of their crisis.

Women often have difficulties with transitions due to fear of change and reluctance to make decisions that they will have to live with. They worry that they will make a mistake and suffer regret, and that keeps them frozen, unable to move. Transitions are necessary to avoid stagnation and along with that process is the need for decisive action. When I teach parenting classes, I often tell moms and dads that the best gift you can give a child is to help her learn how to make decisions. When she's a little kid, standing in the ice cream store agonizing over the right flavor to choose, she needs to summon up the courage to settle on one, and accept it, even if it turns out that her brother's choice is more desirable. Here's the trick: to be able to learn to say to herself, "Next time I'll get the other flavor, but for today, I'll enjoy what I've chosen, even if it's not perfect." It's less important that she makes the right choice than it is that she makes a decisive choice and recognizes that her happiness does not really depend on it.

Women often get lost in details and that hinders us from having movement in life. So let me suggest that if you're the kind of person who gets paralyzed making decisions, don't try to make the exact right decision, but instead, just make any decision and then work with it. That way you will learn that life is flexible and there are many routes to the same destination. I raise this because when a woman is on her own and unused to deciding important things solo, she sometimes gets stuck handling life's challenges. She may look to others to make decisions for her, as if other people know more about her life than she does. Be decisive and avoid dwelling on regret. Once you've made a decision, move on—don't keep making the same decision over and over.

CHAPTER 17

The New Me!

It's no surprise that we're so wedded to the idea that a woman needs a man to be complete. Didn't we all grow up with rescue fairy tales? Remember Cinderella, saved from abuse and drudgery, Sleeping Beauty released from her coma, Snow White returned to life, Rapunzel rescued from the tower, even the Little Mermaid— all turned into respectable gals through the kiss of a prince? So when some warty witch turns our fairy prince into a braying ass and we're spirited back to our lonely tower, you'd think that our first instinct would be to gaze longingly down the forest path, willing the next rescuer to come along.

Screech! Not so fast! Although some women jumped into bed with the first man who came along when their marriages collapsed, most found that the prospect of allowing another man to get close was the furthest thing from their minds. They became what one woman called "born-again virgins." As time went on and they felt healed in many ways, rebuilding trust in men and relationships remained a challenge. Melba's response to my question about how beliefs in the roles of men and women were affected by WAS is typical of many SWAP participants:

> My trust level will never be where it was when I married my husband. I think I realized through this experience that people are unpredictable by nature and there are no sure things on this planet. I would think long and hard about sharing

possessions or homes or families with a man again. I am
very aware of needing an emergency exit to pretty much
everything, available to me at all times. Though I still believe
strongly in commitment and long-term relationships, I'm
much more cautious in how I proceed.

Lynette shares her view but takes it one step further:

It blasted away any romantic vision of marriage for a long
time. I used to think marriage was a place where I could find
shelter from the hardships of the world. Since he left, I worry
that anyone else could repeat his infidelity. After a few years
and a couple of boyfriends, however, I have developed better
boundaries for whom I'll let into my life and have more hope
for sharing my life with someone. It's a conscious effort. I
know I want to give it another try—although it's a struggle.
I'm not looking for marriage. I want a cooperative, joyful,
love-filled, respectful relationship—whatever would work
for me and the other person.

You can hear the caution in both women's statements—how
much they want to be able to trust again and how much fear still
remains. A lot depends on the woman's global assessment of
men—whether she views her ex-husband's behavior as emblem-
atic of all men, or as the particular weakness of that one individual. Here are examples from all parts of the spectrum:

• *Inherent defect in carriers of the XY chromosome*: "I think
  men are basically shallow creatures who can turn their
  emotions on and off like a switch. I will never fully be able
  to trust another man."
• *Defect in this one particular specimen*: "I DON'T believe
  what happened can or should be generalized to 'Well, all
  men are bastards' or anything like that ... This one individual was screwed up and hurtful and obviously such people

DO exist but it's not indicative of the entire male gender being a mess!"
- *Jury's still out*: "I have fleeting thoughts about all men being pigs, but I have a wonderful father and brother, so I know this isn't true."

As indicated by the last statement, much depends on a woman's prior experience with men. If her father was a philanderer, to use a nice old-fashioned word, then her husband's behavior would verify what she *knew* to be true about men—that they're not to be trusted.

Nevertheless, once you've arrived at the **Warm Summer Day Transformational Stage** and you're thinking about taking another chance on love, you'll come face-to-face with the conundrum of dating in the twenty-first century—it's sure changed in the past twenty years and it's going to feel strange. You'll have STDs to deal with, and Viagra, and the daunting prospect of Internet dating. The men who are your age may be looking for women the age of your daughter, and the ones who may be interested in you have one foot in the grave! Laugh! I'm exaggerating! It's not that bad, but it does take courage to get out there again.

The first date I went on was with a nice enough man who had contacted me through an Internet site. On my way to the restaurant where we'd planned to meet one Friday night, I passed all these couples strolling down the street holding hands. Every fiber of my body was rebelling against the coming encounter, and all I could think was, "I want *my* husband." Chatting about my life to this stranger was a Herculean effort. Any topic we touched upon was a minefield. He'd ask, "Have you been to Cape Cod?" "Yes, *we* used to go in the summers." "Did you see such-n-such movie?" "Yes, *we* loved it." "Why did you move to Montreal?" "My *husband* wanted to come to Canada." I was running an emotional marathon and soon hit the wall. I had to excuse myself to go home and cry.

Dating is an important milestone in the recovery process for many women, and whether it happens after six months or six years, it's always going to bring up residual pain. The bizarre feeling I had on that first date slowly faded away when I met other men, until dating no longer felt so strange. I love the saying "What's extraordinary becomes ordinary," and that was the case. I eventually met a man with whom I'm having a relaxed and fulfilling relationship, one that's unlike any other in my life. It's not been about falling madly and passionately in love, but rather about building a deep companionship very slowly over time. SWAP participant 45-year-old Amber, chronicles her progress in the dating realm as follows:

> When I finally felt ready to start dating again, I joined Lavalife. I had several dates with men who were nice (and not so nice), but there was no real connection. However, I had what I call my transition relationship with a very funny and extremely sexy lawyer who made me feel desirable again—and it was a wonderful feeling! He boosted my self-esteem no end by making me feel attractive and smart, neither of which I had felt for a long time. Sadly, he was not interested in a serious relationship, but our two months together were great fun and made me feel good about myself. I met my lovely new man shortly afterwards and we have just celebrated four years together. Meeting him was a major turning point as he made me feel that I could have long-term happiness again. He didn't have children but loves mine, and they in turn adore him.

But, of course, venturing into another serious commitment with a man will not be right for everyone. If you're one of the women who is content with remaining single, or if you want to explore a same-sex relationship, don't let anyone make you feel like you're wrong to not want a man in your life.

This Was Us

As you move into the final stages of your recovery, there are some odds and ends you'll need to deal with—some are tangible and others, more existential. Let's start with the tangible ones—what do you do with stuff? What do you do with jewelry your ex-husband gave you, love letters he wrote you, your marriage certificate, your wedding gown? What do you do with twenty years of photos that documented your life together—your family's life together? What do those things mean now? Do they have value or are they just charred residue that needs to be discarded?

I think every woman has her own answer to that but I'd like to throw in a word of measured caution. Those things were precious once, although right now it hurts to look at them. But years from now, when the pain has all but disappeared, you may be able to sort through them again and retrieve some of their meaning. They are documentation of an important stage in your life. You don't know right now where this bend in the river will take you but it is all part of your journey. It may lead to something good in your future but no matter what, it's part of the whole and you'll need to integrate your marriage and its end into your autobiography.

Mark Knopfler, lead guitarist for the group Dire Straits, wrote a song in 2006 called "This Is Us." It's about a couple poring over the photo album of their life together, reminiscing about all the things they'd done—"This is us in your Daddy's Car ... This is us on our honeymoon ... This is us and our baby boy ... You and me and our memories, This is us." Well, you won't be able to do that with your ex, but you may be able to do it with your kids, or other relatives and friends, later on. So I endorse Julie's approach: "I took all of the things that we had together, pictures and stuff like that, and put it in a box in storage. Everyone told me to burn it, but this was such a long part of my life, why would I not want to remember it at some point. So I just boxed it up and put it away, till I'm ready to go through it."

And I second the noble sentiment that Molly contributed: "Don't throw that wedding ring away or destroy every image of him. That's what he does. You take pride and responsibility for your past—it's your foundation for the future."

And for the more existential odds and ends, what do you do with significant dates and places? What are you going to do with holidays? Are you going to get down in the dumps every year on your anniversary or on the day that he left? Are you going to avoid your favorite restaurant and steer away from parts of town? I think that part of re-empowering yourself is to claw back all facets of your life. You've lost enough—you don't want to keep on losing. Otherwise, every year you will be suffering for a week anticipating your anniversary and dragging yourself through it once it arrives—a waste of a perfectly good day!

Let me suggest that you re-appropriate that day for a better cause. Find out what else happened in history on that day and celebrate it. Maybe it's also Mahatma Gandhi's birthday, so you can wake up that day and wish everyone a happy Gandhi Day. My own husband left on my mother's birthday, so for me, it's easy to mark that day in honor of someone I love. Just don't permit yourself to slip into the blues, year after year. Fight it!

The same with Christmas, Father's Day, Rosh Hashanah and any other celebratory day that you used to spend together. Once you've gotten past the first year or two, don't permit yourself the luxury of wallowing in your misery when you have a holiday to celebrate. Continue your family rituals or figure out new ways to enjoy those days. It'll feel disturbing and odd not to have him there at first, but soon you will get used to it. Use your muscle to make those days great.

And this is important: please don't steer clear of places you would typically go to for fear of running into him. Depending upon how large your town is, it may well happen, but make up your mind that you have nothing to be ashamed of. You're not going to limit yourself just because of old "Gerald." It's your town as well as his, and you're going to enjoy every last inch of it!

You get the drift—adopt a defiant attitude if you must, but keep on living your life! Remember, "It's not about him; it's about you!"

Finally, people may be telling you that you need to forgive to truly heal. I know that forgiving may be close to impossible, so I don't want you feeling like a failure because you can't get there. Here's some advice from Rose about forgiveness:

> It's a ten-gallon word, and the best healing I ever did was when I stopped thinking about the word entirely. It does not apply to my situation. I neither forgive nor don't forgive my husband. You didn't ask for this event, so don't burden yourself with forgiveness. Flying in the face of every self-help book you'll ever read, I will tell you that, in my opinion, it's not necessary to your recovery. Never let anyone pressure you to go there. If it does come, let it come naturally, of its own accord.

The Journey of a Thousand Miles

In the East, the lotus flower is a symbol of transformation. Although its roots grow in a muddy swamp, its flower pushes inches above the surface of the water in stark white loveliness. The lesson of the lotus flower is that we can transcend ugliness and suffering and create beauty in this world. SWAP participant Priscilla sent me this quote from Eva Jessye, the first black woman to receive international distinction as a professional choral conductor, back in the early twentieth century. The subject of the quote is regret: "You should not suffer the past. You should be able to wear it like a loose garment, take it off and let it drop." If only it were so easy. But maybe, as time goes on, the past will shape-shift so that it eventually assumes a different, less hostile form. We may begin to be able to retrieve pleasure in the good of the marriage along with the pain of its untimely demise. Like Georgia, who came to accept that the watch she got from her husband as a wedding present served as a reminder of something that was once good in her life, we will become able to sift out the bad and preserve the good. And one day, you may be able to say to him in your mind: *"Thank you for being the agent of my transformation!"*

Peg describes some aspects of the transformation that has taken place in her life as a result of her husband's departure six years ago:

> I eventually started my own communications firm with two other women. It's been the experience of a lifetime and I never would have done it if I'd been married. I've also recently returned to music as a hobby, and have forged ahead with that further than I've ever gone. I play with other musicians around Wichita, which has opened up the city to me. I now know hundreds of people. I would not have gone this far with my music if I'd stayed married to him.

Mary Jo also feels positive about her new life and is very proud of herself. Five years post-WAS, she has an understanding boyfriend with whom she's had a child and bought a house.

> I can see just how amazing I am for forging through and refusing to let the experience define me or my life, for keeping in mind what I wanted, what was important, and still taking risks (emotional ones, especially) so that I could achieve those dreams and have the life I wanted. I've inherited a bunch of other problems, of course (whose life is without problems?), but I have more confidence in my ability to deal with them. And it's made me a much, much better mother and partner than I was/would have been before. A better person, I think. Still, let's face it—I would have much preferred to learn these "lessons" some other way.

Although some women who participated in the Sudden Wife Abandonment Project believe that they will never fully recover, most, like Peg and Mary Jo, feel that they've moved on. "It is like healing after a major surgery. The pain may be gone, but the scar is still there." But if we take that analogy one step further, like a necessary surgery, the scar may represent a new chance at a healthier life. You didn't know that there was something unhealthy growing inside, but it's been removed and now you have a lot of life to live.

For me, the point at which I felt that my life had settled into a "new normal" occurred about two and a half years out. I've learned so much about life and have changed in measurable ways. Perhaps the most profound way is that I've chosen to embrace a stress-free lifestyle. I often have feelings of happiness and am filled with appreciation for everything and everyone in my life. The new me is very comfortable with where I am and expects that that sense of comfort will only increase. That's not to say that it doesn't still hurt to think about how happy I was in my marriage or about my ex-husband's betrayal—it does. But I don't think of that as a bad thing—just as a feature of my life.

There is an old Chinese saying, "The journey of a thousand miles begins with a single step." This quote from Lao Tzu reminds us that no matter how great a distance we want to cover, in order to get where we're going, we have to start where we are.

Take the first step in front of you and then the next and the next, and if you just keep going, you will eventually arrive at your destination. But … do you know where your destination is? No, no, don't look back—look forward! *It's not about him; it's about you.* Where are you *headed*? Where would you like your life to be in five years? What do *you* want to accomplish? Think that through but keep it uncomplicated and do-able. What would make you proud of yourself? It doesn't have to be a grand scheme, just one that you're sure you can make happen. And the key to most successes in life is so very simple—just keep going. Like Nathalie, you will eventually make it over the finish line.

Nathalie's story

The second summer after my husband had left, I got involved in marathon paddling—racing long distances in 40-pound Kevlar racing canoes using 7-ounce paddles. A friend had asked me at a gathering during the winter if I paddled. She suggested that we train together in the spring to see if I liked racing. We did and I loved it. During long-distance training runs, I would moan and groan to her about my sadness and sorrow over his leaving. She herself had had a horrible divorce some years previous. She used to say, "By the time you get to Dawson City (746 km down the river), you'll have washed that man right out of your hair."

I did eventually learn not to look back because if I did, I couldn't keep the damn boat straight. The physical exercise and workout were such a help to me at that point in my grieving. I put everything of myself into that boat and into those races—it helped me forget for a little while. At that time, the sheer raw physical paddling rhythm and speed saved me. Six years later, I'm still racing and have the honor of holding the fastest women's time in the longest canoe and kayak race in the world.

The river and the paddling made such a great impact on me—it was one paddle at a time, just like one day at a time. Who could ever (I sure couldn't) imagine a race starting with the first paddle stroke and reaching Dawson City 746 km later? I did it, one paddle stroke at a time. There is no magic formula, just keep going, eventually you will get there, the sadness WILL lift.

Thank you for letting me guide you as your Sherpa on part of your journey. I know that you have come a long way from your starting point when you opened this book for the first time. I'm sure that some tears have been shed. But I hope there were also times when your heart lifted up in anticipation of the good things to come in your life. You know now that you're not alone—many other women who have experienced Wife Abandonment Syndrome are walking alongside you. I believe in you and know that you can take control of your future and that you will soon meet the new, renewed you.

What Happily Married Women Need to Know

You'll be happy to hear that quite a good percentage of Sudden Wife Abandonment Project participants entered into happy marriages following Wife Abandonment Syndrome. Come to think of it, very few talked about a subsequent marriage becoming a disaster. Women who have been abandoned learned a lot about healthy relationships that women in long-term marriages may not know. So, to determine if your marriage might be headed toward WAS, ask yourself about these warning signs:

- Has your husband had affairs in the past or left previous relationships in a similar way? That's the strongest predictor that he has what it takes to do it again.
- Does he seem suddenly unhappy with his life, even if the complaints he is raising are not related to your marriage? It's a sign that he may be rethinking things.
- Do you notice a personality change? Does he just not seem himself? Is he withdrawn or suddenly irritable? Is he snapping at the children or not wanting to participate in family activities?
- Are his habits changing—things like suddenly going to the gym, buying new clothes, dying his hair, getting a tattoo, buying an expensive car?
- Do his values seem to be in flux? Is he adopting ideas that he used to belittle or belittling things he used to value? Is he espousing new beliefs that surprise you?

- Is he taking mysterious business trips or disappearing for periods of time and the reasons given just don't seem to make sense to you?
- Has he started to frequently mention a woman at work, telling you about her in an innocent way?
- Does he work in a career in which he is in a position of power or authority, such as a professor, pastor, or business executive where young women may look up to him?

The biggest thing that SWAP participants know that women in long-term marriages don't is that WAS is possible. Many times women in my therapy practice have discounted very obvious signs, saying, "My husband would never have an affair. I know him. He just wouldn't." Men who are suddenly irritated at every little thing their wife does while extolling the virtues of some woman at the office. Men who are staying out at the sports bar till 4 a.m. after watching the hockey game, which ended at 11 p.m., and then cannot be reached because their cell phone was turned off. Men who had been impossible to pry out of the same old pair of sweat pants who suddenly insist on a closet full of designer labels. Women who have been through it once would know immediately that something is not right. It takes courage but you need to open yourself to the possibility that if the signs are there, your husband may be having an affair. Take a deep breath and look at it squarely.

So what can a woman do to preserve a healthy marriage if she is not getting those obvious warning signs? Two things—first, check in with him from time to time and ask, "How're we doing?" Many women hit with abandonment were so sure that everything was fine that they never bothered to enquire. Second, take whatever complaints your husband raises seriously. Sometimes, either the husband minimizes his complaints or the issues raised seem so trivial that the wife doesn't realize how important they are to him.

The SWAP study included questionnaires completed by some runaway husbands themselves, and here Jonathan provides a fascinating explanation of the dynamics of his marriage of eleven years prior to his leaving:

What I learned through all this is that when a couple says they never fight, it's probably a bad sign. We never fought either. I believe the problem is that men and women communicate for different purposes. Women tend to talk about problems or issues with the desire to talk through things and feel validated. Men tend to talk to solve problems (not saying which is better, that's just the way it seems to be). So when I expressed my views and nothing changed I just started to shut down after a while and stop caring.

Men tend to talk sparingly about how they feel, but when they do speak, they are looking for something to happen. My wife said, "Why didn't you scream at me if you were upset and I wasn't listening?" I felt all along that if I was saying something, then she should be listening, and that listening should lead to some action of some sort.

Particularly after decades together, people in long-term marriages often assume that they know the other one so well, they don't need to do any profound thinking about their partner's reality. I suppose that comes under the heading of taking someone for granted. Runaway husbands may have voiced their concerns very timidly, so any unhappiness they had with the marriage was really not evident to the wife. Jonathan's wife had said, "Why didn't you scream at me if you were upset?" The answer is that he had checked out emotionally and she was clueless.

Women can protect themselves in marriage by making sure that they are living a well-peopled life. We all need relationships on various levels so that if the marriage falls apart, or even if your husband dies unexpectedly, you have others in your life who are already part of your support network. I'm a great believer in the value of friendships, and co-workers and neighbors can also lend a hand or give an encouraging pat on the back (remember my neighbors and the chiming silver heart!)

Women should also be well versed about the family's financial situation and have some means in place for being able to support themselves. Wives need to know how to do the essential things required for running a household—banking, car maintenance and so on. Those old days in which a woman could depend on her husband to manage all the concrete tasks involved in making a home run smoothly are long gone.

Sudden Wife Abandonment Project Questionnaire

Hi! I'm a family therapist and researcher who is studying Wife Abandonment Syndrome—the devastating experience of being told by your husband that the marriage or long-term relationship is over when you had no idea there were even problems. The purpose of the study is to explore the possible motivation for men to abandon their wives without forewarning, to understand the feelings that result, and learn how women cope and recover from the experience.

By completing and returning the questionnaire, you indicate your agreement for your answers to be used in the preparation and promotion of a book on the topic. Please be assured that your identity will not be revealed.

In order to participate, you must fulfill the following criteria:

- You are a woman who was in a long-term live-in relationship.
- You believed that your marriage/relationship was relatively healthy.
- You were unaware that your partner was planning to leave until the moment that it happened.
- The marriage/relationship ended quickly.

I greatly appreciate your participation in this study and hope that you will find the experience of telling your story liberating and healing. Before you start, get a glass of water or something to drink, put on some nice music and settle in to learn something new about the end of your marriage—and remember to breathe!

Many thanks!
Vikki Stark, M.S.W.

1 Your city, state or province? How did you hear of this Study?
2 Your current age and occupation.
3 Age and occupation of your former partner.
4 How long were you married or living together?
5 How long ago did your relationship end?
6 Any children together or from a previous relationship? What were their ages at the time of the ending of your marriage?
7 How would you have described your marriage prior to learning that it was over?
8 To what extent did you and your spouse discuss your relationship and what areas of conflict were there?
9 How would you have described your former spouse's personality?
10 Please tell the story, in detail, of how you were informed and the reasons you were given for the end of the relationship.
11 Do you remember what you thought and felt on hearing the news?
12 How long after you learned that the relationship was over did one of you move out?
13 During the first six or eight months, which emotions did you feel most often? (Despair, rage, obsession, fear, depression, shame, relief, regret, irritation, tolerance, resolution, confusion, hatred, traumatized, longing, loneliness, others?)
14 How did you deal with the pain?
15 Did you have fantasies of revenge or did you actually *do* something to try to hurt your former partner?

16 What was the hardest part—the darkest place you went to inside?

17 What was the craziest thing you did?

18 Were there any turning points in your recovery process?

19 Were you physically affected by being left? Weight change, insomnia, health problems, anti-depressants, overdrinking or drug use, risky behavior, other?

20 What is your theory about why your husband left the way he did?

21 Has this experience changed how you feel about yourself? How so?

22 What has it done to your image of the marriage you thought you had?

23 Has it affected your beliefs about human beings and the world, in general? Beliefs about women or men?

24 What was your former husband's relationship like with his mother growing up?

25 What was your former husband's relationship like with his father growing up?

26 To what extent would you say you were a caretaker in your relationship?

27 Thinking back now, can you see signs that it was coming? What were they?

28 Did the timing coincide with any particular significant event in your lives?

29 If there was an affair involved, how did you find out? How did the fact that there was an affair affect you? How would you describe the affair partner?

30 If you have children, how have they been involved? How have they been affected?

31 Please tell in detail what specific things friends and family said or did that helped or hurt? What role have they played?

32 Did you go for therapy? Did you feel your therapist understood what you were going through?

33 What kinds of things did you do or tell yourself to make it through? What was healing for you? Any tricks that helped?

34 Were there positive things about the ending of your relationship? If so, at what point did you recognize that?
35 How has your life changed since it happened?
36 Any advice for other women who have recently been left?
37 What is your relationship with your former husband like now?
38 Do you feel you've recovered fully and moved on?
39 Would you take him back?
40 Anything else to add?

Thank You!

Now, take a few deep breaths and let your mind go to something in your life that brings you joy.

Take good care of yourself!

Songs that Helped SWAP Participants Make it Through

"2 the Left" by Beyoncé

"Before He Cheats" by Carrie Underwood

"Better Things" by The Kinks

"Big Girls Don't Cry" by Fergie

"Billy" by James Blunt

"Change" by Tracy Chapman

"Closer to Fine" album by The Indigo Girls

"Every Rose Has Its Thorn" by Poison

"Far Away" by Nickelback

"Gone, Gone, Gone" by Robert Plant and Allison Klauss

"Goodbye My Lover" by James Blunt

"Hallelujah" by Leonard Cohen

"Hit 'Em Up Style" by Blu Cantrell

"I Will Survive" by Gloria Gaynor

"I'm Still Standing" by Elton John

"Just Can't Last" by Natalie Merchant

"Karma" by Alicia Keys

"Landslide" by The Dixie Chicks

"Last Day of Our Acquaintance" by Sinéad O'Connor

"Leave (Get Out)" by Jojo

"Life is Sweet" by Natalie Merchant

"Me" by Paula Cole

"Monkey Wrench" by Foo Fighters

"Morphine" by The Rolling Stones

"My Happy Ending" by Avril Lavigne
"My Immortal" by Evanescence
"Never Again" by Pink
"Not In This Life" by Natalie Merchant
"Not Ready to Make Nice" by The Dixie Chicks
"Off the Hook" by Barenaked Ladies
"On My Own" by Patti LaBelle
"On My Own" by Whitney Houston
"Only a Memory" by Garth Brooks
"Over You" by Chris Daughtry
"Pictures" by Sheryl Crow
"Question" by The Moody Blues
"Right Now" by Carrie Underwood
"Since U Been Gone" by Kelly Clarkson
"Smile" by Lily Allen
"Strength, Courage and Wisdom" by India Arie
"Taking the Long Way" by The Dixie Chicks
"Tubthumping" by Chumbawamba
"Water of Love" by Dire Straits
"White Flag" by Dido
"Why" by Annie Lennox
"Wild Women Don't Get the Blues" by Lyle Lovett
"You Learn" by Alanis Morrisette
"You Oughta Know" by Alanis Morrisette
"You Were Meant for Me" by Jewel
"Your Love is a Lie" by Simple Plan
"You've Got a Friend" by Carole King

Join the Community of Women Helping Women

Now you can be part of The Sudden Wife Abandonment Project! Visit my website at www.runawayhusbands.com – the resource center for helping women recover from Wife Abandonment Syndrome. You can read what other women have to say and add your own unique story.

I look forward to hearing from you!

www.runawayhusbands.com

Index

LaVergne, TN USA
02 April 2010
178032LV00003B/296/P